SUPPORTING SUCCESS FOR

TOOLS FOR INCLUSIVE CAMPUS PRACTICE

CINDY ANN KILGO

Cite as:

Kilgo, C. A. (2020). *Supporting success for LGBTQ+ Students: Tools for inclusive campus practice.* University of South Carolina, National Resource Center for The First-Year Experience & Students in Transition.

ISBN: 978-1-942072-33-1
ISBN (ePub): 978-1-942072-34-8
ISBN (eBrary): 978-1-942072-35-5

Published by:
National Resource Center for The First-Year Experience® and Students in Transition
University of South Carolina
1728 College Street, Columbia, SC 29208
www.sc.edu/fye

The First-Year Experience® is a service mark of the University of South Carolina. A license may be granted upon written request to use the term "The First-Year Experience." This license is not transferable without written approval of the University of South Carolina.

Production Staff for the National Resource Center:
Project Manager: Tracy L. Skipper, Assistant Director for Publications
Design and Production: Krista Larson, Graphic Artist
External Reviewers: Peter Arthur, University of British Columbia
                             Lisa Marie Kerr, University of Alabama at Birmingham

---

Library of Congress Cataloging-in-Publication Data

Names: Kilgo, Cindy A., author.
Title: Supporting success for LGBTQ+ students : tools for inclusive campus
   practice / Cindy Ann Kilgo.
Description: Columbia : National Resource Center for The First-Year
   Experience and Students in Transition, University of South Carolina, 2019.
   | Includes bibliographical references.
Identifiers: LCCN 2019022252 (print) | LCCN 2019002301 (ebook) | ISBN
   9781942072331 (pbk.) | ISBN 9781942072348 (Epub) | ISBN 9781942072355
   (Ebrary)
Subjects: LCSH: Sexual minority college students--Services for--United
   States. | Homosexuality and education--United States.
Classification: LCC LC2574.6 .K55 2019 (ebook) | LCC LC2574.6 (print) | DDC
   371.826/60973--dc23
LC record available at https://lccn.loc.gov/2019022252

About the Publisher

The National Resource Center for The First-Year Experience and Students in Transition was born out of the success of University of South Carolina's much-honored University 101 course and a series of annual conferences focused on the freshman year experience. The momentum created by the educators attending these early conferences paved the way for the development of the National Resource Center, which was established at the University of South Carolina in 1986. As the National Resource Center broadened its focus to include other significant student transitions in higher education, it underwent several name changes, adopting the National Resource Center for The First-Year Experience and Students in Transition in 1998.

Today, the Center collaborates with its institutional partner, University 101 Programs, in pursuit of its mission to advance and support efforts to improve student learning and transitions into and through higher education. We achieve this mission by providing opportunities for the exchange of practical and scholarly information as well as the discussion of trends and issues in our field through convening conferences and other professional development events such as institutes, workshops, and online learning opportunities; publishing scholarly practice books, research reports, a peer-reviewed journal, electronic newsletters, and guides; generating, supporting, and disseminating research and scholarship; hosting visiting scholars; and maintaining several online channels for resource sharing and communication, including a dynamic website, list-servs, and social media outlets.

The National Resource Center serves as the trusted expert, internationally recognized leader, and clearinghouse for scholarship, policy, and best practice for all postsecondary student transitions.

Institutional Home

The National Resource Center is located at the University of South Carolina's (UofSC) flagship campus in Columbia. Chartered in 1801, UofSC Columbia's mission is twofold: to establish and maintain excellence in its student population, faculty, academic programs, living and learning environment, technological infrastructure, library resources, research and scholarship, public and private support and endowment; and to enhance the industrial, economic, and cultural potential of the state. The Columbia campus offers 324 degree programs through its 15 degree-granting colleges and schools. In fiscal year 2019, faculty generated $279 million in funding for research, outreach and training programs. South Carolina is one of only 32 public universities receiving both Research and Community Engagement designations from the Carnegie Foundation.

Contents

Tables and Figures

Tables

Figures

Preface

This book aims to serve as a one-stop resource for faculty and staff in higher education settings who are seeking to enhance their campus climate and systems of support for LGBTQ+ student success. Specifically, the volume includes theoretical frameworks and conceptual models that can be used in practice. Using the synthesis and critique of existing literature and analyses of data from the Campus Pride Index, I explore the role of specific functional areas in supporting LGBTQ+ students as they transition into, move through, and exit collegiate contexts. I also include guiding questions for practitioners to consider when evaluating the resources and climate for LGBTQ+ students within various functional areas on campus.

Throughout the text, I provide examples of inclusive excellence at institutions in the United States. These examples are based on Squire and Beck's (2016) *Developmental Pathways to Trans Inclusion on College Campuses*. Within their monograph, the authors described three additive steps toward inclusive practice, with inclusive excellence as the culminating step, which they define as the development of programs, polices, and practices that are universally trans-affirmative. It is my hope that this book equips higher education professionals with tools for creating LGBTQ+ inclusive and affirming environments on their campuses.

As a starting point, I want to take the opportunity to share how I navigated higher education as a person who holds both minoritized gender and sexual identities. I offer this in an effort to be transparent about my identities and lived experiences as I interpret and synthesize the existing literature, analyze data on LGBTQ+ issues, and provide recommendations for practice. I also share the ways I navigated these minoritized identities within my own work in higher education. It is my hope that this narrative provides additional context in the form of one person's experiences with inclusivity on a college campus.

My Personal Narrative

I spent my teenage years living in a highly conservative, rural, and deeply Christian area of Georgia. I attended public K-12 schools, yet the schools in this area had very overt Christian emphases (i.e., marching band holding crosses during half-time performances, teachers praying openly in school). It was also a highly segregated community. For context, my senior year of high school was the first year that the homecoming court was desegregated. School tracking was present, as well, with student placement in college prep, technical prep, or career prep differing significantly by race and socioeconomic status. Within this context, being anything but heterosexual was not only seen as very bad, but it was a source of intense bullying.

Reflecting back, I remember many moments where my sexual orientation was brought into question in ways that were harmful. Sometime in late junior high, students began talking about me being gay. I remember sitting in a classroom, having notes passed between people on all sides of me. I could see comments about me on top of these notes. I remember whispers in the hallways. I remember teammates not giving me a hug in celebration of a huge play or win. I especially remember one moment when a teammate gave me a high five after a double play. Another teammate went up to her and whispered that I was gay, so not to high five me again.

At that time in my life, I am not sure if I knew fully what my sexuality was. I did know, however, that I did not want to be gay. I constantly denied any claim otherwise. I was heavily involved in a church youth group, where there were frequent lessons on why being gay was a sin. Someone even claimed, during a small group discussion, that being gay was worse than any other sin and argued that a popular song "promoted" that sinful lifestyle. They thought this was a worse influence for youth than other songs we discussed that day.

I finally had a tipping point one day in class, when the notes, the whispers, and the laughter kept coming. I remember not being able to control my tears. Before I knew it, I was sobbing in science class, which wasn't a good look for anyone at that age. My teacher took me into the hallway to determine what was happening. I remember telling her about what people were saying. I will never forget what she did next. She asked to pray over me and then proceeded to pray aloud that I would not go toward "deviant" lifestyles. As a result of these and other experiences during that part of my life, I ultimately repressed any idea that I was gay. I did everything I could to convince anyone who would listen that I wasn't gay, and I waited for the day when I could leave that K-12 environment.

As a college undergraduate, I distinctly remember walking by the Gay–Straight Alliance student organization meetings in the student union, glancing in, but being too afraid to actually go in. I was actively involved on campus, holding several student leader roles and jobs. Being a student worker and heavily involved in student affairs activities, I was viscerally fearful of entering the Gay–Straight Alliance space—partially because I felt at that time that it would be equivalent to outing myself. Having grown up in a community that equated being gay with the "worst sin I could commit," my second-year self couldn't consider going that route. College had been my escape from the harmful rhetoric and extensive bullying, but college had also been a place where I repressed my identities more than ever before. I was fearful of reverting back to my K-12 experiences by walking into the Gay–Straight Alliance meeting.

I eventually entered that space. After walking back and forth by the room, one of the people I knew from my involvement on campus—and who was openly out as gay—walked out of the room and said, "You know you can come in here if you want." I knew this person but had never spoken to him. I took his invitation, however, and finally walked in. The queer community I eventually built in college allowed me to continue to gain more confidence and self-acceptance of my varied identities. I eventually came out to this community. The time I had in college, in community with other LGBTQ+ people for the first time in my life, changed my awareness of my sexual identity in an affirming way.

College was also a time when I experienced discrimination that changed the path of my career and life. In one of my campus roles, I attended regular meetings with other students. Several of my peers were using homophobic language within the space. A few of my peers and I brought this up several times in group discussion. The student affairs professional present could not conceptualize why I, as someone not fully out in this particular setting, would be so upset about the homophobic language. Of course, this was highly problematic, in and of itself. One night, the person continued to ask me why I was so upset. It was relentless. "But, Cindy Ann, why are YOU upset?" "But, why?" I finally escaped the conversation by exasperatingly exclaiming, "Because I am gay!" The student affairs professional had accomplished getting the answer they wanted. They also shared this news with others. Things were rocky for me in that group setting for a while. I will never know the intent this person had, but their repeated questions about my investment in ending the use of homophobic language and then outing me to others caused me immense pain.

After this incident, I found support from several other student affairs professionals. They affirmed my identity—the first time anyone had done so outside of my peers from college. I also had empowering moments with two faculty members, in particular, who allowed me to explore my sexual identity through class writing assignments. They both encouraged me to explore my identities while affirming my existence and providing constructive feedback on my work. In the moment, I did not realize how much of an impact those interactions had, but in retrospect, they were a defining part of my collegiate experience. They created a positive image of an identity that had always been demeaned by other authority figures in my life. Instead of producing shame, the events that resulted built my self-acceptance and carried me through the rest of my undergraduate years.

I did not know it at the time, but the experience of being outed by a student affairs staff member during my undergraduate study was the impetus for my career. As an actively involved undergraduate, I eventually learned that student affairs was an entire career field. I had no concept of it in that way until one of my mentors asked if I had considered it. I eventually found the field of higher education (and student affairs, in particular) an ideal trajectory to be a positive force for other queer students. I desperately wanted to be a staff member who affirmed students' identities, as the staff who affirmed mine had such a large influence on my life and well-being. I never want another student to experience being outed by a staff member. I want LGBTQ+ students to exist in a collegiate environment where it is not scary to walk into an LGBTQ+ student organization meeting. I want LGBTQ+ students to succeed and thrive alongside their cisgender and heterosexual peers.

I eventually enrolled in graduate school at a different institution in the Southeast for my master's degree, followed by a midwestern institution for my doctoral degree. During my time as a graduate student, I continued to grapple with my identity. I was fairly comfortable as openly queer, but I was internalizing my gender identity and expression. I continued with this internal battle until my third year of doctoral study. I will never forget the space, the moment, where I was able to speak my truth. I was at a professional conference with several others from my institution, and I attended a session on trans identities. During the session, I participated in an activity for trans people. It was the first time I had shared with anyone else that I was genderqueer. Later that day, I asked one of my mentors from my doctoral institution to meet briefly before a reception. We sat on the convention center stairs as I stumbled through the conversation, eventually blurting out that I was genderqueer. The best thing ever happened next: She affirmed my identity, told me she was proud of me, asked what she could do to be there for me (particularly with pronouns), and gave me a hug. Her response was unlike any I had ever experienced. It brought me to tears, and for once, those tears were accompanied by joy and relief.

Once back on campus, I met with her again to get her insight on how to tell my other mentors about my identity and how I wanted to be addressed. She encouraged me to email them, as the institution did not have an option for listing identity-aligned pronouns within student records at that time. So, I drafted the emails, which she graciously offered to review, and sat on them for a few weeks until I finally felt strong enough to click "send." In reflection, it is hard to believe I struggled for so long to send them. My doctoral program was relatively small and had vocalized strong support for inclusion and justice, and my experiences outside the program itself were limited to mostly research courses I took in other colleges.

My previous experiences working with undergraduates at the University of Iowa, however, led me to consider what this experience would have been like if I didn't know my faculty so closely. I worked for a year, during my doctoral study, with undergraduate students who were seeking research opportunities on campus. This largely involved meeting with interested students and helping them find faculty members to reach out to with inquiries for research opportunities. Before each meeting, I pulled up the student's record to learn basic details: their major, their classes and credit hours earned, and their academic standing. When I pulled up a record, it would show me a photo of the student from their ID card, their legal name, and the abovementioned information I needed before the meeting. What I found, however, was that the records system was greatly limited in that it did not include a student's chosen name or pronouns. Given this knowledge, I began asking students for their names and pronouns. If I had not asked, a student whose name might not match their record would have to out themselves to me before we even had a chance to establish any kind of rapport. This idea was problematic and gave me great pause. The stress I felt in disclosing my identity to my few, trusted doctoral faculty was completely unlike the experiences of undergraduate students, who had many more faculty and staff interactions than I did. After reflecting on the experiences that the undergraduate students with whom I met had to grapple with and then my own coming out experience, I wished for a more inclusive system—one that allowed students to fully and accurately represent themselves, without burden, to faculty, staff, and peers.

It is important to note that my other identities, particularly those that hold privilege, greatly influenced my collegiate experience, departure from college, and current work. As a White, cisgender-passing person, my experience was radically different from students who hold minoritized sexual and gender identities alongside additional minoritized social identities, particularly race. While I share my personal story as a preface to this book, I cannot do so without acknowledging the violent and often radically different experiences that LGBTQ+ people of color experience in navigating the same spaces and systems I navigated and continue to navigate. This is a critical point and caution as I share my story. When considering the experiences that LGBTQ+ students have within higher education, it is essential that their other social identities are acknowledged. The LGBTQ+ population is far from a monolith and should not be treated as such when working with students on campus.

My career has been built on studying the ways college affects students and on preparing professionals to enter higher education equipped to not only work with LGBTQ+ students and others with minoritized identities but also to affirm and promote the success of these student populations. After my experience coming out as genderqueer during my doctoral study, I sought ways to relieve the burden placed on students to disclose their pronouns within college contexts. During my last year of doctoral study, I worked with a mentor and others on campus to transform the institutional records at our institution to alleviate the burden of continual disclosure that students faced.

Specifically, we worked to decouple sex and gender from my institution's admissions application, include pronouns, and have this information fed into the student records system to which faculty and staff have access. To make pronouns a normalized part of the student record, alongside students' identification numbers, academic majors, and contact information, we sought to have them placed on the main student records page (i.e., the first one faculty and staff see when accessing a student's record). Along with others, I audited all restrooms on campus and sought funding for new, consistent signage to be placed on all gender-inclusive restrooms. I worked to create a website on trans issues at the institution, with resources and information for the campus and local community. My last effort was to propose a university-wide task force to continue to advocate for trans students, faculty, and staff. The proposal was accepted and eventually commissioned by the institution. Even beyond my postsecondary experiences, I continue to study this population of students and create institutional change related to the success of LGBTQ+ students.

When the opportunity arose for me to write this book, I was very excited to put forth recommendations for transforming college environments to be queer and trans inclusive. No higher education institution is perfect, nor is there one checklist for any institution to become *inclusive.* At the same time, however, there are many opportunities for faculty and practitioners to create welcoming and affirming environments for students who hold minoritized gender or sexual identities. This book is not meant to serve as a blueprint for campus inclusion; rather, I hope it provokes thought and reflection about how each reader may individually transform their own practices to meet the needs of LGBTQ+ students. One important thing that I have learned through navigating higher education as both a student and a scholar is that there are so many practices—minor though they may seem in the grand scheme of things—that are actually quite remarkable in creating inclusive environments for students. I encourage each reader to carefully consider the guiding questions posed in this text. Inclusive environments are built by people, and each person on a college campus has a role in that.

Acknowledgments

In writing this text, I have several people who I wish to acknowledge for assisting me in this process. First, I wish to thank the National Resource Center for The First-Year Experience and Students in Transition and in particular, the volume editor, Tracy Skipper. I am appreciative of the opportunity to work with the Center to write this important volume and am thankful for the patience and guidance of Tracy and others in helping prepare this text for publication. I also wish to thank my colleagues in the Higher Education Administration program at The University of Alabama for their support and encouragement of me writing this volume. In particular, I wish to thank the two department chairs while I was writing this text, Claire Major and Frankie Santos Laanan. I also wish to thank my colleagues Karri Holley and Steve D. Mobley, Jr., for their encouragement and feedback during the writing process. There are several graduate students who assisted me with various tasks related to this book. In alphabetical order, I thank Lauren Bennett, Chavada Davis, Kit Emslie, and Pat Reynolds. I appreciate not only your help with gathering sources, checking references, and organizing articles, but also with challenging me to think in different ways while writing this volume. I wish to thank my mentor-turned-friend, Jodi Linley, and my dear friend, Jaime Shook Miller, for their continual support and encouragement of this work. Finally, I want to thank the UA College of Education Writing Force group. Thank you, Kristine Jolivette, for coordinating this group, and for the entire group for cheering me on as I finished sections and helping me troubleshoot when I came across writing struggles. Your constant encouragement and celebration have allowed me to finish this volume.

Chapter 1

Introduction

A decade ago, a large-scale study (Rankin et al., 2010) found the college campus climate for lesbian, gay, bisexual, trans, and queer (LGBTQ+) students was bleak. Since that publication, at the time the largest such study focused on LGBTQ+ college students, other researchers have found similarly negative campus conditions. Their findings include perceptions of unwelcoming and at times hostile climates in the classroom (Furrow, 2012; Garvey & Rankin, 2015), within specific institutional contexts (Garvey et al., 2015; Rockenbach & Crandall, 2016; Zamani-Gallaher & Choudhuri, 2016), for students who hold specific social identities (Garvey, Sanders et al., 2017; Rockenbach et al., 2017; Vaccaro, 2012; Woodford et al., 2017), and within international contexts (Okanlawon, 2017).

Going further, several studies suggested such a climate has an adverse effect on students' psychological and physical health, as well as their career development (Schmidt et al., 2011; Woodford & Kulick, 2015; Woodford et al., 2015; Woodford et al., 2014). More recent research, however, has framed LGBTQ+ students as succeeding despite these negative factors. This line of inquiry has focused on how this group succeeds through resilience (Alessi et al., 2017; Nicolazzo, 2016a; Nicolazzo, 2016b; Walker & Longmire-Avital, 2013).

Institutions of higher education play a critical role in LGBTQ+ student success, as it does for all students. While emerging research focuses on how colleges and universities can support this group (Pitcher et al., 2018), institutions have historically worked to purge these students from campus (see Wright, 2006). In recent years, however, many have created programs and initiated efforts geared toward supporting LGBTQ+ students (Cramer & Ford, 2011; Fine, 2012). Further, within student affairs, professional competencies guide practitioners toward inclusive action on campus. The College Student Educators International (ACPA) and Student Affairs Administrators in Higher Education's (NASPA) (2015) professional competency of Social Justice and Inclusion specifically focuses on "meet[ing] the needs of all groups, equitably distributing resources, raising social consciousness, and repairing past and current harms of campus communities" (p. 14). While this professional competency does not address the needs of students who hold minoritized, or oppressed, sexual and gender identities exclusively, LGBTQ+ students are one of many groups for whom issues of access and equity should be addressed.

In approaching this book on inclusive practices that support the college success of LGBTQ+ students, I have analyzed the research literature published on this population since 2010 and examined current institutional practices. My goal in undertaking this study is two-fold. First, I hope to offer insight into the needs of LGBTQ+ students and the unique conditions related to their success in college. I also seek to highlight exemplary policies and practices that can guide professionals who are seeking to create inclusive learning environments not just for LGBTQ+ students but for all students on their campus. In this chapter, I define terms related to sex, gender, and sexual identity used in the research and practice literature to create a baseline of understanding. I also briefly touch on what it means to hold both privileged and oppressed identities simultaneously. Finally, I offer some insight into my approach to engaging the research and practice literature and how it shaped the organization of this book.

Understanding the Intersections of Gender and Sexuality

At the basic level of understanding, three terms that are critically different, yet often conflated are (a) sex, (b) gender, and (c) sexual identity. In both scholarship and practice, these terms are used interchangeably and in aggregate (Renn, 2007). These terms are also conflated within the media, as well, which complicates and sometimes even minimizes certain identities. I begin this volume by defining some terminology that is common across LGBTQ+ identities. While language is ever evolving, it is important to have a shared understanding in approaching this topic.

Sex and Gender

The terms *sex* and *gender* are often conflated. Sex, unlike gender, corresponds to the biological identity a person has, including their chromosomes (Patton et al., 2016; Stryker, 2008). Example categories of sex include female, intersex, and male. Nicolazzo (2016b) noted that Western thought characterizes gender "as a naturalized, immutable fact that is always already tethered to one's assigned sex at birth" (p. 166). This connection between gender and sex has led to frequent interchangeable usage within society at large and specifically within higher education. When official forms ask students to select a *gender*, yet the options for gender include sex categories (i.e., often on the binary of male or female), gender and sex are being conflated.

Scholars have noted gender as both a cultural phenomenon (Stryker, 2008) and the way people "identify, express, and embody the socially ascribed norms relating to their assigned sex at birth" (Nicolazzo, 2016b, p. 166). There are two overarching categories of gender: transgender and cisgender. *Transgender* is an umbrella term for people whose gender identity differs from the sex they were assigned at birth (Rubin et al., 2016). *Trans* is an abbreviated form of transgender, used as a prefix or adjective (e.g., a trans person; Rubin et al., 2016). *Cisgender* is an umbrella term for someone who identifies with a gender identity that corresponds to the sex they were assigned at birth. Additionally, *Cis* is an abbreviated form of cisgender, used as a prefix or adjective (e.g., a cis person; Rubin et al., 2016). Transgender and cisgender are examples of gender identities, which also can include androgyne, demigender, genderqueer, man, trans, and woman, among others (see Table 1.1).

Table 1.1
Defining Gender

Term	Definition
Agender	An umbrella term that encompasses many gender identities. Often, agender people do not identify with any gender. They may define their gender as neutral or non-binary (Braquet, 2019).
Androgyne	Noun form of *androgynous,* referring to people who identify or present as neither distingu shably male nor distinguishably female (Calvacante, 2019).
Demigender	An umbrella term for identities that only partially adhere to binary definitions of gender. The terms *demiboy* and *demigirl* are sometimes used as nouns associated with the adjectival *demigender* (Calvacante, 2019).
Genderqueer	A term generally used for people whose gender identity or gender expression do not operate within the gender binary. As such, genderqueer may encompass a number of different gender identities/expressions. Comparable—but not necessarily interchangeable—terms include *non-binary, genderfluid,* and *gender-nonconforming* (Calvacante, 2019).
Man	According to a binary understanding of gender, the noun used for any person who identifies primarily, or exclusively, as male (Rubin et al., 2016). Both cis and trans people can identify as men.
Queer	An umbrella term for people of minoritized sexual or gender identities who are not heterosexual or cisgender. The term has a complicated history as a reclaimed slur (Braquet, 2019).
Two Spirit	A term used to "describe Native Americans who are on a spectrum of genders and sexualities, thus inhabiting both masculine and feminine traits" (Braquet, 2019, p. 53).
Woman	According to a binary understanding of gender, the noun used for any person who identifies primarily, or exclusively, as female (Nagoshi et al., 2019). Both cis and trans people can identify as women.

Gender pronouns are another important consideration. Pronouns (e.g., they, she, ze, he) are used to reference people. Within the English language, pronouns have various forms (reflexive, possessive, object) and can be used in the first, second, or third person. With using gender pronouns in this context, however, we focus on third person. There are many gender pronouns that exist. Further, some people do not use gender pronouns, but instead substitute their name in place of a pronoun.

Referring to someone by the correct pronouns is very important. When meeting new people, introductions that include chosen pronouns allow individuals to refer to new acquaintances correctly in future contexts. If everyone introduces themselves with their chosen pronouns, a normalization of correct pronoun usage occurs. It is also important to know that sometimes people change their pronouns. Later in this text, I discuss ways that colleges can alter their student records to allow students to accurately update their pronouns.

Sexuality and Gender

Sexuality and gender are two distinct aspects of identity. A person's sexual identity corresponds to both their attraction and desire for people based on gender and sex as well as their acknowledgement of that attraction and desire (Patton et al., 2016). Some examples of sexual identities include bisexual, gay, lesbian, pansexual, queer, same gender-loving, and heterosexual (see Table 1.2). A person can hold one sexuality or gender, multiple sexualities or genders, or can be *asexual* or *agender* (holding no sexual identity or gender). When events are publicized to LGBTQ+ student populations but are not designed to be inclusive of trans identities, sexual identity and gender are being conflated.

Another useful term related to both gender and sexuality is *coming out*, which refers to the process by which an individual identifies and accepts their minoritized sexual or gender identity. As GLAAD (n.d.) notes, "publicly sharing one's identity may or may not be part of coming out" (para. 15). In other words, a person's coming out is not solely their disclosure to others. It is also very important to note that one's level of outness is often based on many factors, including personal safety. As Garvey, Mobley, et al. (2019) state, "being 'out' is a privilege that many QTPOC students are not often afforded, especially when compared with White queer and trans* individuals" (p. 151).[1] A person's depth of coming out does not define their identity.

Acronyms

The terms defined in this section allow one to understand the myriad sexual and gender identities that students hold, as well as understand the specific letters within acronyms to describe the LGBTQ+ population. As previously mentioned, gender and sexual identity are often conflated into one acronym (e.g., LGBT), despite the distinct differences between the two forms of identity (Renn, 2007). Further, acronyms used to describe this population vary considerably. Table 1.3 includes a list of commonly used acronyms to describe this subpopulation of students.

Given the various acronyms used to describe this subpopulation, how does one know which term to use? A primary consideration is ensuring that the acronym appropriately defines the subpopulation being examined or referenced. For example, during a program examining the intersection of sexual identity and religion, a facilitator might want to use *LGBQ+* or *LGBQA+* to describe sexual identities separate from gender or sex (i.e., T and I). At times, however, practitioners are concerned with sexual identity and gender (e.g., a

---

[1] QTPOC stands for queer and trans people of color. See Table 1.3.

Table 1.2
Defining Sexual Identity

Term	Definition
Asexual	A term for people who do not experience sexual attraction. *Asexual* or *ace* is an umbrella term that includes several other identities (Mollet, 2020).
Bisexual	A person who experiences sexual or emotional attraction to more than one gender. Some argue that the term bisexual is declining in popularity because of its implication that gender operates solely in a binary existence (Trans Student Educational Resources, n.d.). This argument, however, is nuanced by others who reinforce that bisexuality is not exclusive to the gender binary but rather is attraction to more than one gender (Bowerman, 2016; Burns, 2016).
Gay	A person who is romantically, sexually, or emotionally attracted to members of the same gender. Often applied primarily to cisgender men, this term can be used to indicate same-gender attraction regardless of a person's gender identity/expression (Braquet, 2019).
Heterosexual	Adjective for the emotional, romantic, and/or physical attraction to members of the "opposite" gender (Braquet, 2019).
Lesbian	A term referring to a woman who experiences romantic, sexual, or emotional attraction to other women (Calvacante, 2019).
Pansexual	A term for people who can experience sexual, emotional, or romantic attraction toward people of many/any sexual and gender identities (Braquet, 2019). The term pansexual is not new but has recently emerged as a gender-inclusive term encompassing all genders (Burns, 2016).
Queer	An umbrella term for people who ascribe to nonnormative, minoritized gender and sexual identities (Calvacante, 2019). Historically, a sexual slur, the term has now been reclaimed by some LGBT people (Braquet, 2019).
Same gender-loving	A term used to indicate attraction to, or love for, members of the same gender. Often used instead of gay or lesbian to recognize that gender is not binary (Braquet, 2019).

queer- and trans-inclusive sexual health workshop). In these cases, it is appropriate to use acronyms that include all of those identities (i.e., LGBT, LGBTQ+, LGBTQIA+). Another consideration is that, as noted above, sometimes the letters can be attributed to different groups (i.e., queer or questioning). With regards to the letters being attributed to asexual or ally, Mollet and Lackman (2018) shared that asexual students felt erased by having ally within the acronym. It is important to be specific and intentional in use of acronyms, considering who is included and who might be excluded before using one.

Table 1.3
Acronyms and Symbols

Acronym	Terms within acronym/meaning of symbol
LGB	Lesbian, gay, bisexual
LGBT	Lesbian, gay, bisexual, and transgender
LGBTQ	Lesbian, gay, bisexual, transgender, and queer or questioning
LGBTQIA	Lesbian, gay, bisexual, transgender, queer or questioning, intersex, and asexual or ally
QTPOC	Queer and trans people of color
+	As a suffix, symbolizes more (i.e., not all identities are represented within the acronym listed)
*	As a suffix, used by some scholars to signify that trans represents more than just trans women and men. There is debate on the use of the asterisk within the trans community (Tompkins, 2014).

Within this text, I use the acronym *LGBTQ+* to describe minoritized gender and sexual identities in aggregate. If I am describing minoritized gender and sexual identities individually, I will use the term *trans* and acronym *LGBQ+*, respectively. When describing or referencing literature on students minoritized by gender and sexual identities, I will use the terminology from the original source.

Privilege and Oppression

When discussing topics related to gender and sexuality, it is important to consider the environments in which people who hold minoritized gender and sexual identities are situated. First, however, we must take a step back and explore the concept of systemic oppression and how it privileges and marginalizes different subpopulations of people.

Watt (2015) defined systemic oppression as "a comprehensive set of interrelated attitudes and behaviors that are normalized that position dominant and oppressed groups in a power dynamic" (p. 14; see also Hardiman et al., 2007; Pharr, 1997). Using the term *minoritized identities*, Linley (2017) suggested certain identities are "rendered minority status based on others' perceptions of [those] identities or systems that favor privileged identities (see Benitez, 2010; Osei-Kofi, Shahjahan, & Patton, 2010; Stewart, 2013)" (p. 643). Within society, systems of oppression continue to perpetuate privilege and marginalization based on sexual orientation, gender, and sex. For example, some may assume that oppression toward LGBTQ+ people has been eradicated with the U.S. Supreme Court's decision upholding marriage equality, yet LGBTQ+ people still experience oppression of their sexual and gender identities. This population still faces barriers getting accurate identification documents, adopting children, and dealing with discrimination and harassment in the workplace, to cite a few examples.[2] Trans people are significantly more likely to attempt suicide than the population as a whole and face increased violence within U.S. society (James et al., 2016). LGB youth are disproportionately incarcerated and tend to be imprisoned longer than their heterosexual peers (Wilson et al., 2017). LGBTQ+ people may also lack access to basic resources, such as public restroom facilities (James et al., 2016).

Queer theory offers a framework for exploring privilege and oppression. It stems from poststructuralism and focuses on the fluidity and social construction of gender and sexuality (Butler, 1990). According to Abes and Kasch (2007), "queer theory critically analyzes the meaning of identity, focusing on intersections of identities and resisting oppressive social constructions of sexual orientation and gender" (p. 620). In other words, queer theory works to break down the oppressive systems that perpetuate privilege and minoritize some groups. Students who hold minoritized sexual or gender identities experience *heterosexism*, *genderism*, *homophobia*, and *transphobia*. Table 1.4 includes definitions of terms specific to oppression of people who hold minoritized sexual or gender identities.

Watt (2015) noted that higher education is a microcosm of the larger society. The impetus for this book is built around identifying and dismantling the ways that higher education institutions, whether intentionally or not, oppress and minoritize LGBTQ+ students. Preston and Hoffman (2015) described this in their conceptual model of the traditionally heterogendered institution, which they argued is "an institution that, despite the desire to create programs supporting LGBTQ students, upholds and promotes a heterogendered discourse through institutional structures and foundation" (p. 82). I encourage readers to be cognizant of their own identities and how those may uphold privilege and marginalization as they move throughout the book and think about ways to support LGBTQ+ students. The following questions offer a useful starting point:

- Do my sex, gender, and sexual identities hold privilege or marginalization within U.S. society?

- How do my privileged and/or minoritized identities shape the ways I engage with the content of this book?

- How do my identities shape the ways I am aware of issues faced by LGBTQ+ students on my campus?

- How do my identities shape the ways I interact with LGBTQ+ students on campus?

---

[2] In June 2020, the U.S. Supreme Court, in ruling on two separate cases, affirmed that Title VII of the Civil Rights Act affords employment protections to LGBTQ+ individuals.

Table 1.4
Defining Oppression of LGBTQ+ Identities

Term	Definition
Allonormativity	"The societal influence that perpetuates allosexuality [people who experience sexual attraction] as universal" (Mollet, 2020, p. 189)
Cisgenderism	The ideology "that denies, denigrates, or pathologizes self-identified gender identities that do not align with assigned gender at birth as well as resulting behavior, expression, and community" (Lennon & Mistler, 2014, p. 63)
Deadnaming	When a person uses a birth or legal name for a trans person, rather than the person's chosen name (Knutson et al., 2019)
Genderism	Enforcement of a gender binary (Nicolazzo, 2016a)
Heteronormativity	"An assumption, by individuals or in institutions, that everyone is heterosexual, and that heterosexuality is a superior orientation" (Braquet, 2019, p. 54)
Heterosexism	The ideology that denies and rejects people who identify as other than heterosexual (Woodford et al., 2018)
Homophobia	Fear and hatred of people with minoritized sexual identities (Nagoshi et al., 2019)
Misgendering	The use of a pronoun, honorific, or term that is incorrect for a person (Braquet, 2019)
Transnormativity	The concept that "all trans* people should transition from one socially knowable sex to another (e.g., male-to-female)" (Nicolazzo, 2016b, p. 1175)
Transphobia	Fear and hatred of trans people (Rubin et al., 2016)

Overview of the Book

Student success in college has been a longstanding outcome for postsecondary education (Kuh et al., 2005; Mayhew et al., 2016; Pascarella & Terenzini, 2005). Common developmental tasks during the college years—finding purpose, developing identity, managing emotions, becoming reflective thinkers, and developing moral reasoning to name a few—are both facilitators and hallmarks of college student success. Yet, student development theory began with studies focused on students who hold power in society (i.e., White, male, high socioeconomic status)—what Jones and Stewart (2016) identified as the first wave of student development theory. In their analysis, the "second wave" began focusing on minoritized identities, followed by the "third wave" that focused on the systemic oppression that marginalizes certain groups (Jones & Stewart, 2016, p. 21). Understanding this evolution is critical in reframing markers of student success for LGBTQ+ student populations.

A Guiding Frame: Renn's (2010) Status of the Field

In 2010, Kristen Renn published a pivotal report, "LGBT and Queer Research in Higher Education: The State and Status of the Field," that summarized the limited existing literature on queer and trans people. She categorized her findings into three content areas: "[a] visibility, [b] campus climate, and [c] identity studies" (2010, p. 136). Renn described visibility as having evolved from studies in the early 1990s that illustrated LGBTQ+ student narratives, based on their increasing presence on campuses, to the emergence of research describing multiple and intersecting identities in the late 2000s. The characterization of campus climate encompassed three components: "[a] perceptions and experiences of LGBT people, [b] perceptions about LGBT people and their experiences, and [c] the status of policies and programs designed to improve the academic, living, and work experiences of LGBT people on campus" (p. 134). Finally, Renn described identity studies as scholarship that incorporates a wide range of methods, both qualitative and quantitative, to explore and examine gender and sexual identities. In Chapter 2, I examine and categorize the literature since 2010, focusing on its usefulness for faculty and staff working with LGBTQ+ students on college campuses. The chapter also provides a brief resource guide for emerging theories and conceptual models specific to LGBTQ+ students.

Exploring Inclusion on Campus

Increasing awareness of the challenges queer and trans students face in higher education, and of the need for stable and supportive collegiate environments that serve these students' needs, has necessitated LGBTQ+ inclusivity instruments and measures on campus. Researchers have noted the variety of strategic interventions for meeting the needs of these diverse communities (Ivory, 2012; Pitcher et al., 2018; Rankin & Garvey, 2015; Renn, 2010). Further, as Pitcher et al. (2018) noted, not all interventions have empirical backing (including the effectiveness of inclusive policies). This makes evaluating institutions' level of inclusiveness (based on the interventions and policies at an institution) of their queer and trans constituents difficult at best.

To understand more about inclusion efforts, I rely on data from the publicly available Campus Pride Index of LGBTQ-Friendly Colleges and Universities (herein referred to as the Campus Pride Index or CPI), a free online index (Campus Pride, 2018) that illustrates current issues and trends within LGBTQ+ resources and policies. Campus Pride describes itself as "the leading national nonprofit organization for student leaders and campus groups working to create safer, more LGBTQ-friendly learning environments at colleges and universities" (Campus Pride, n.d.-a, para. 2).[3] The goal of the Campus Pride

---

[3]Campus Pride specifically uses *LGBTQ* to describe lesbian, gay, bisexual, transgender, queer, and questioning people within its index (Campus Pride, n.d.-b). When referencing data from the Campus Pride Index, I use LGBTQ to be consistent with their language.

Index, created in 2001, is to serve as "a valuable national assessment tool for campuses looking for ways to improve their LGBTQ campus life" (Campus Pride, n.d.-b, para. 1).

The Campus Pride Index is an opt-in dataset in which institutional representatives report their college or university's policies and practices across a wide array of functional areas. The Index is composed of eight LGBTQ-friendly measures: policy inclusion, support and institutional commitment, academic life, student life, housing and residence life, campus safety, counseling and health, and recruitment and retention (Campus Pride, n.d.-a). Response to items on the index are strictly yes or no (i.e., an institution has or does not have a policy, practice, or resource) and does not ask about students' perceptions of campus climate. According to the organization's website, the Campus Pride Index has been used since 2001, with a large update in 2015 (Campus Pride, n.d.-b).

Use of Campus Pride Index data. While the Campus Pride Index is updated as more institutions provide data, I only used publicly available institutional information from two-year and four-year, public and private not-for-profit institutions reporting as of February 2018. The total number of institutions included within my analyses is 299. I created a spreadsheet with data within each measure listed on the Campus Pride Index for all institutions in the sample and created individual variables for each item within each measure (43 total variables). If an institution had the measure included, I coded *yes* as 1 and *no* as 0. I then used Excel to conduct the descriptive analyses reported on throughout the book. It is important to note that I only include aggregate, descriptive analyses in this text. The Campus Pride Index is updated consistently as more institutions submit their data. Additional information can be gathered on institutions through the Campus Pride website (http://campusprideindex.org).

Limitations. The nature of the Campus Pride Index significantly limits the inferential utility of the data it generates. My sample of higher education institutions from the Campus Pride Index is less than 10% of the total colleges and universities in the United States. Because the instrument hinges on self-assessment by colleges and university representatives, only those representatives can vouch for the accuracy and completeness of the data reported, thus calling into question the empirical soundness of these findings. The Campus Pride Index relies on the institutional knowledge of the representative doing the reporting; thus, the limits of that knowledge constrain the accuracy of the data collected. Campus Pride addresses this by stating that the representative should be an employee in an official capacity to represent the university and/or work with LGBTQ campus issues (Campus Pride, n.d.-b).

It also stands to reason that the institutions doing little to support their LGBTQ constituents would be less likely to self-report on their inclusivity efforts (or lack thereof). As a result, a researcher or practitioner accessing the data might conclude that the absence of an institution implied a lack of inclusivity measures being practiced on that campus. Such a conclusion is not necessarily accurate, however, as the institution might not have self-reported for other reasons (e.g., scarcity of resources, lack of information about the Campus Pride Index).

In sum, while the Campus Pride Index may prove useful for describing the trajectory of LGBTQ inclusivity efforts within U.S. collegiate contexts, it is neither exhaustive nor objective in the information it makes available. I provide these critiques to clarify that any inferences made using Campus Pride Index data must be qualified with the understanding that this index represents only "a necessary first step" in advocating for LGBTQ individuals in higher education in the United States (Campus Pride, n.d.-a).

In Chapters 3 through 5, a synthesis of the relevant literature is followed by inclusive excellence examples drawn from the Campus Pride Index and campus case studies and guiding questions for specific functional areas. Chapter 3, for example, covers literature on LGBTQ+ students' anticipatory and early socialization and entry into college followed by institutional examples of inclusive excellence during the early college experience. The final section of the chapter provides questions to guide higher education professionals on creating inclusive environments for LGBTQ+ students within three functional areas: admissions and registrar offices, orientation, and first-year programming.

Chapter 4 focuses on curricular and cocurricular spaces within higher education. The first section gives an overview of campus climate literature and specific experiences LGBTQ+ students have within and beyond the classroom. The second section provides institutional examples of inclusive excellence across a range of institutional contexts and environments. The third section relays guiding questions for creating inclusive environments for LGBTQ+ students within student leadership programs, campus ministries, student recreation, and classroom engagement.

In Chapter 5, I explore the transition out of college for LGBTQ+ students by reviewing the literature on career and employment-related issues for LGBTQ+ populations and LGBTQ+ alumni engagement. Inclusive excellence examples and guiding questions focus on career services, retention and college outcomes, and alumni engagement.

Chapter 6 serves as the book's conclusion, offering a brief overview of relevant institutional change models that can be used in a variety of campus contexts. This chapter ends with a call to action for higher education professionals related to both individual growth and the creation of policy and practices inclusive of and affirming to LGBTQ+ students in collegiate contexts.

Chapter 2

The State of Higher Education for LGBTQ+ Students: An Update

Renn's (2010) review of queer and trans literature catalyzed scholars to revisit the experiences of LGBTQ+ people in higher education. While investigating this new scholarship, I reviewed many publications focused on LGBTQ+ college students. I also found theoretical/conceptual models developed since 2010 that relate specifically to this population. Many aspects of the literature remain the same, including the three broad categorizations Renn outlined: (a) visibility, (b) campus climate, and (c) identity studies/experiences. However, two additional categories have emerged: (a) studies centered on a variety of outcomes specifically for queer and trans college students and (b) studies focused on LGBTQ+ education programs.

Following is a broad overview and analysis of the literature published since 2010, organized into the three categories Renn (2010) put forth and the two that emerged from my own review. This chapter is not intended to delve into individual studies, but rather to ground the book with literature presented since 2010. Figure 2.1 shows the five broad categories of scholarship on the subject, along with subcategories I have created for each.

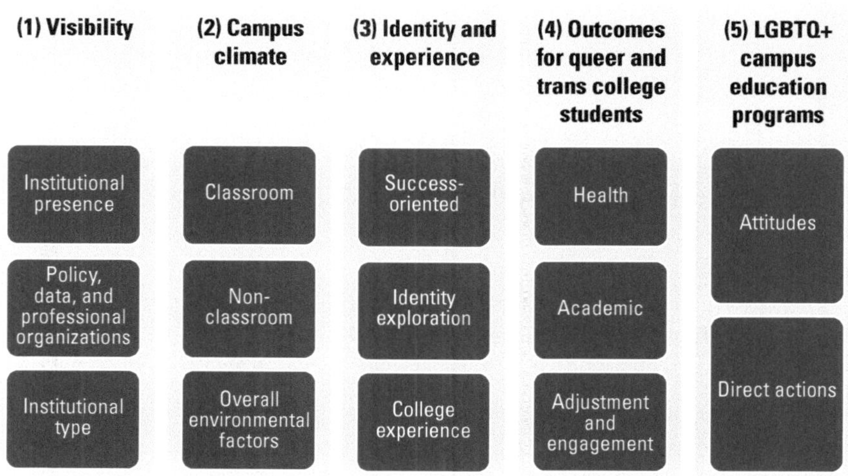

Figure 2.1. Synthesis of higher education LGBTQ+ literature since 2010. Categories 1-3 first appeared in Renn's (2010) analysis of the literature, with subcategories added. Some publications can be classified within multiple categories and subcategories.

Visibility

Renn's (2010) characterization of visibility in the research literature was related to the increase in presence of queer and trans students in higher education. Since 2010 the notion of visibility has broadened, encompassing three subcategories: (a) institutional presence; (b) policy, data, and professional associations; and (c) institution type. Within my review, institutional presence relates to the increased efforts on campus to support LGBTQ+ students and the presence of out LGBTQ+ students on campus and as alumnx.[4] The second subcategory —policy, data, and professional associations—describes the presence of LGBTQ+ identities within institutional policy, research focused on college students, and national higher education conferences. Institution type reflects both the lack of recognition of LGBTQ+ people historically within various types of institutions and of their emerging presence within those institutions.

Institutional Presence

Studies in this subcategory included recruitment of LGBTQ+ students. For example, Cegler (2012) and Young (2011) both described the increased efforts to recruit LGBQ+ students, while Newhouse (2013) noted the lack of targeted recruitment for transgender collegians. Mathis and Tremblay (2010) noted the use of websites, specifically, in increasing recruitment efforts. The subcategory also included the increased presence of an on-campus LGBT resource centers as well as a critique of LGBTQ+ support services that centered cisgender and/or White identities (Marine & Nicolazzo, 2014; Self & Hudson, 2015). Fine's (2012) study suggested prestigious, public institutions in more liberal regions were most likely to have an LGBTQ+ resource center. Other studies in this subcategory illustrated the increased presence of LGBTQ+ topics and identities within cocurricular settings, particularly the need for more work at the department level (Bazarsky et al., 2015), and also in curricular settings, including medical education/training (Davy et al., 2015). Finally, research on alumnx giving has suggested that student involvement is a predictor for LGBTQ+ students' giving (Garvey, 2016) and that community uplift is important for LGBTQ+ alumnx engagement (Garvey & Drezner, 2013).

Policy, Data, and Professional Organizations

Studies in this subcategory focused on trans-specific policies, including both the National Collegiate Athletic Association (NCAA)'s policy for transgender athletes (Bowden & McCauley, 2016) and the use of deficit-based language in institutional policies intended to support trans students (Dirks, 2016). This category also included a broader discourse on how to identify and classify queer and trans identities within higher education research, with

---

[4]Alumnx is a gender-inclusive term used purposefully to dissociate the gender binary (Garvey & Drezner, 2019).

inclusion of LGBTQ+ identity markers (Beemyn & Brauer, 2015; Brauer, 2017; Crowhurst & Emslie, 2014), the need to look beyond a sexual identity binary and separate groups out (i.e., lesbian, queer, gay; Dugan & Yurman, 2011; Garvey, 2017; Rankin & Garvey, 2015), and the utility of the Campus Pride Index for campus administrators (Garvey, Rankin et al., 2017). Finally, Pryor and colleagues (2017) illustrated how the College Student Educators International (ACPA) and National Student Affairs Professionals Association (NASPA) have increased the prevalence of LGBTQ+ topics within conference presentations, with themes including visibility, identity, and campus climate.

Institution Type

This final subcategory stressed the lack of literature on queer and trans populations within certain institutional types: specifically historically Black colleges and universities (HBCUs; Mobley & Johnson, 2015), community colleges (Beemyn, 2012; Nguyen et al., 2018; Ottenritter, 2012; Taylor et al., 2018; Zamani-Gallaher, 2017; Zamani-Gallaher & Choudhuri, 2011, 2016), religiously affiliated institutions (McEntarfer, 2011; Rockenbach & Crandall, 2016), and women's colleges (Hart & Lester, 2011). This literature posited that queer and trans students not only exist in all of these institutions but also that their on-campus visibility is increasing.

Campus Climate

Campus climate arguably is the area LGBTQ+ higher education scholars have scrutinized most thoroughly (Renn, 2010). Vaccaro (2012) described the variation in definitions of campus climate, including students' perceptions, attitudes and behavior of campus community members, and a combination of psychological, behavior, organizational, and historical components (Kuh, 1990; Rankin & Reason, 2008; Milem et al., 2005). Within this text, I rely on Vaccaro's wide description of campus climate with regard to the ways in which LGBT students experience the institution environment.

The campus climate studies published since 2010 fall into three subcategories: (a) classroom-specific; (b) non-classroom; and (c) overall environmental factors. The first subcategory, classroom-specific, included studies that focused on experiences that LGBTQ+ students have within curricular spaces on campus. In these studies, a negative environment was illustrated for trans students (Pryor, 2015) and for gender-nonconforming students compared to their gender-conforming peers (Garvey & Rankin, 2015). Furrow (2012), whose study examined English composition courses, also illustrated a negative learning environment for LGBT students and asserted that faculty are responsible for creating safe environments for students in their classrooms. The second subcategory, non-classroom experiences, included studies examining the prevalence and influence of perceptions of a negative campus environment. Studies in this subcategory suggested that

Black gay male undergraduate students face multiple forms of discrimination (Strayhorn & Mullins, 2012) and that negative climates can limit students' career development (Schmidt et al., 2011) and mediate the effects of undergraduate research on LGBQ+ students' academic development (Kilgo et al., 2019).

The final subcategory, overall environmental factors, included studies on both institution type and aspects of climate not specifically defined by in-class or out-of-class spaces. Studies in this subcategory explored climates at community colleges (Garvey et al., 2015; Taylor, 2015; Zamani-Gallaher & Choudhuri, 2011, 2016), Christian higher education institutions (Hughes, 2018a; Rockenbach & Crandall, 2016), and "traditionally heterogendered institutions" (Preston & Hoffman, 2015, p. 64). Together, these studies suggest that the campus climate is still as bleak for LGBTQ+ students, across all institution types, as reported in earlier research. Further, studies that had a broader campus perspective also illustrated similar overall negative perceptions of climate, including across generational and time-specific perceptions of climate (Beemyn & Rankin, 2011; Garvey, Sanders et al., 2017), organizational perspectives of climate (Pitcher et al., 2018), campus climate and religion (Rockenbach et al., 2016, 2017), microclimates (Vaccaro, 2012; Woodford et al., 2017), experiential climate (Woodford & Kulick, 2015; Woodford et al., 2015), and homophobia and heterosexism (Friedman & Leaper, 2010; Okanlawon, 2017; Rankin et al., 2010; Woodford, Kulick et al., 2014).

Identity and Experience

More recent literature has focused on student success and resilience, offering counternarratives to the often-negative experiences that LGBTQ+ students reported in earlier studies (Rankin et al., 2010). For example, Pitcher et al. (2018) used organizational analysis to highlight the positive campus climate trans students experienced. Their study examined students' perceptions of climate but also their sources of support on campus. The researchers found that students relied on LGBTQ resource centers, student organizations, and the existence of trans-inclusive policy as sources of support (Pitcher et al., 2018). They also noted that not all students described campus climate as negative, with some taking a positive view and others classifying it as neutral (i.e., "indicated by describing an absence of negative events;" Pitcher et al., 2018, p. 126). These findings suggest that negative perceptions of climate are not a foregone conclusion as earlier research might have suggested.

Pitcher et al.'s (2018) study was not the only one suggesting progress for LGBTQ+ students regarding campus climate. Nicolazzo et al. (2017) explored the concept of kinship specifically for trans students, finding that trans* kinship—a form of relationship similar to kinship to family of origin, but related specifically to trans kin or family—promoted success for this group. Nicolazzo (2016a, 2016b) similarly found kinship and resilience as important to trans students' success in college. These studies all suggest that while some campus environments are perceived as negative, LGBTQ+ students are resilient in navigating these heteronormative spaces in ways that lead to personal and academic success. Further, these studies illustrate the recent shift away from studies focusing exclusively on campus climate to those focusing more broadly on sexual and gender identity development, and LGBTQ+ student success in postsecondary contexts.

Identity Exploration

Studies in this subcategory explored gender or sexual identity in concert with other identity statuses or as an independent identity. This included studies centered on men or males, including Black gay men in marching bands (Carter, 2013), non-heterosexual men (Dilley, 2010), spiritual gay and bisexual Black men (Means, 2017), and sexual minority males (Tillapaugh, 2015). Other subpopulations of focus within this subcategory included queer women (Friedman & Leaper, 2010), queer and trans people with disabilities (Miller, 2015, 2017), trans and gender non-conforming students (Beemyn & Rankin, 2016), and queer and trans students of color (Duran, 2018; Nicolazzo, 2016c). Additional studies focused on sexual identity development (Denton, 2016) and the leadership identity development of queer students (Olive, 2015). Studies also focused on queer performativity (Hart & Lester, 2011; Waling & Roffee, 2017), a concept put forth by Butler (1990, 2014) that involves gender as an action rather than a stagnant concept.

College Experience

Several topics emerged within the college experience subcategory, including the first-year experience and transition to college (Alessi et al., 2017; Baum, 2012; Cegler, 2012; Jackson, 2016; Squire & Norris, 2014), the experiences of trans collegians specifically (Beemyn & Rankin, 2016; Dugan et al., 2012; Duran & Nicolazzo, 2017), the experiences of Black non-binary trans students (Nicolazzo, 2016c), experiences with student services and functional areas on campus (Krum et al., 2013; Pryor et al., 2016; Rockenbach et al., 2016; Schulze & Perkins, 2017; Strayhorn & Mullins, 2012), classroom or faculty interaction experiences (Furrow, 2012; Garvey & Inkelas, 2012; Hughes, 2017; Linley & Nguyen, 2015; Linley et al., 2016; Pryor, 2015), activists' experiences (Githens, 2012), student organizations (McEntarfer, 2011), experiences predicting identity salience (Hughes & Hurtado, 2018), and experiences at community colleges (Zamani-Gallaher & Choudhuri, 2016) and at women's colleges (Hart & Lester, 2011).

Outcomes for Queer and Trans College Students

A number of studies since 2010 have examined outcomes for queer and trans collegians, moving beyond outcomes related to identity and climate experiences on campus. These outcomes can be organized into three areas: (a) health, (b) academics, and (c) adjustment to college.

Health Outcomes

The mental health of LGBTQ+ students was the focus of multiple studies (Grant et al., 2014; Johnson et al., 2013; Woodford et al., 2015, 2017, 2018). Among these studies, several found that heterosexism and microaggressions targeted toward LGBTQ+ students led to increased risk for mental health conditions and suicide. In particular, Grant et al. (2014) found that within a one-institution sample, LGBQ students had increased risk for depression and lower self-esteem than their heterosexual peers. Johnson et al. (2013) pushed for the necessity of campus support for LGBT students given increased suicide rates. Woodford et al. (2015) found similarly negative mental health outcomes among LGBQ students; however, these findings were predicted by heterosexist harassment. Another study by Woodford et al. (2018) looked at the role of microaggressions for both cisgender LGBQ and transgender students. For the LGBQ sample, these microaggressions predicted an increased risk for suicide. Within the trans sample, microaggressions predicted increased risk for depression. Resilience mediated the relationship between microaggressions and suicide among the LGBQ student sample.

Related to mental health outcomes is the use of alcohol and drugs. Both Manning et al. (2012) and Woodford et al. (2015) investigated alcohol and drug (AOD) use among LGBTQ+ students. Manning et al.'s study investigated the resources on 10 college campuses and found that institutions overall lacked AOD and other health resources, including LGBTQ+ resources. Woodford et al. (2015) found that while heterosexism increased the risk for alcohol abuse, having LGB friendships moderated that effect.

Several scholars have highlighted the resilience of LGBTQ+ students (Alessi et al., 2017; Nicolazzo, 2016a, 2016b; Walker & Longmire-Avital, 2013). Nicolazzo's (2016a, 2016b) and Alessi et al.'s (2017) work highlight the role that resiliency has on transgender students' navigation through college, despite the systemic barriers presented by society. Additionally, Walker and Longmire-Avital (2013) found that among their sample of Black LGB young adults, faith and religion was a coping mechanism for participants who also reported high levels of internalized homophobia. These findings collectively suggest that queer and trans students are exhibiting resiliency to navigate systemic oppression.

Academic Outcomes

Other studies explored what I have defined as academic outcomes. These include cognitive skills (Dugan et al., 2012), retention (Fine, 2015; Hughes, 2018b; Sanlo & Espinoza, 2012), satisfaction with faculty and staff interactions (Garvey & Inkelas, 2012; Linley et al., 2016), career development (Schmidt et al., 2011), developmental challenges

(Woodford et al., 2017), and academic integration (Woodford & Kulick, 2015). These studies illustrate some negative findings for LGBTQ+ students.

Dugan et al. (2012) used data from the Multi-Institutional Study of Leadership (MSL) to examine a variety of outcomes for transgender, LGB, and cisgender-heterosexual students. Their study found that trans students had lower reported gains in cognitive skills than their LGB or cisgender-heterosexual peers. They attributed this to possibly lower self-esteem levels among trans students. Using data from the National Longitudinal Survey of Adolescent Health, Fine (2015) investigated the role of gender and sexuality on retention, finding that sexual minority women were the least likely in the study to have completed college. Fine's study contradicts earlier literature suggesting that both women and LGB persons were more likely to complete college than their peers who identified as men or heterosexual. Finally, Hughes (2018b) also found a negative academic outcome for sexual minority students, with a decreased retention rate within STEM fields compared to their heterosexual peers. These studies illustrate the need for faculty and practitioners to consider the academic effects that LGBTQ+ students might face due to negative campus climate.

Garvey and Inkelas (2012) explored college students' perceived satisfaction with faculty and staff interactions, finding that LGB students were more satisfied than their heterosexual peers, though the effect size was small. Linley and colleagues (2016) found that the role of supportive and affirming faculty is critical for students. While academic outcomes may be negatively affected by transphobia and homophobia on campuses, faculty and practitioners can serve as support systems for LGBTQ+ students.

Adjustment to College

Limited research exists on the transition and adjustment to college for LGBTQ+ students. Alessi and colleagues (2017) found that engagement in LGBQQ student organizations, friendships with LGBQQ students, and opportunities for identity expression on campus were important for students in their sample. Kirsch and colleagues (2015) found that LGB students experienced increased distress that influenced their psychosocial transition throughout college. Despite the increased distress, however, their findings suggested that college administrators can provide psychoeducational resources for LGB students. Both of these studies point to the need for more research on the transition to and adjustment in college for LGBTQ+ students and for campuses to respond to LGBTQ+ students in ways that facilitate their adjustment.

LGBTQ+ Campus Education Programs

The scholarship published on LGBTQ+ campus education programs since 2010 consists of literature on various perceptions of queer and trans people and on the direct action educators and students can take to create inclusive campus environments.

Attitudes Toward LGBTQ+ People

The first subcategory specifically relates to studies on attitudes held by a variety of campus stakeholders. Researchers have highlighted ways that campus units can reinforce or create transphobia and homophobia (Wickens & Sandlin, 2010). Marine and Nicolazzo (2014) explored the conflict between the LGBTQ+ resource centers and trans-inclusion, highlighting that homophobia and transphobia persist even within structures designed to support LGBTQ+ inclusion.

Several scholars have examined attitudes based on a variety of markers, including social identity predictors (e.g., religious identity, sex, and friendship) with LGBTQ+ people, among others (Deniz, 2017; Wolff et al., 2012; Woodford et al., 2012) and attitudes from Greek-affiliated groups and student athletes (Worthen, 2014). These studies reify a negative campus climate and also illustrate pockets of campus where practitioners need to focus education efforts.

Direct Actions to Create Inclusive Environments

The second subcategory relates to action, as opposed to strictly attitudes, and includes studies related to grassroots activism within higher education and student affairs (Githens, 2012; Martin et al., 2018); statewide networks to support LGBTQ+ efforts (Cramer & Ford, 2011); advocacy for LGBTQ+ curriculum inclusion within medical school training (Davy et al., 2015); supporting LGBTQ youth (Beemyn, 2015); bystander intervention (Dessel et al., 2017); the role of faculty and staff at community colleges in creating cocurricular opportunities and an inclusive campus environment (Ivory, 2012; Ottenritter, 2012; White et al., 2012); coalition-building between communities (Rivera-Ramos et al., 2015); the role of teaching assistants in including LGBTQ+ topics within the classroom (Jaekel, 2016); non-discrimination policies (Case et al., 2012); creation of LGBTQ+ student organizations, learning communities, and student support groups (Jaekel, 2015; McEntarfer, 2011; Vespone, 2016); and ally training (Woodford et al., 2014; Worthen, 2011). These studies are the next step for the attitudes and beliefs that society holds about LGBTQ+ identities. They suggest that faculty and practitioners have a role to play in creating a more affirming and accepting campus environment for LGBTQ+ students.

Theories and Models

The theoretical and conceptual models for sexual and gender identity development and for supporting LGBTQ+ college students have changed dramatically over the past decade. Previously, lifespan development models pervaded the higher education and student affairs literature (Patton et al., 2016). In recent years, however, scholars have critiqued and problematized several of these models (Bilodeau & Renn, 2005; Garvey et al., 2018; Patton et al., 2016), arguing that they do not adequately represent the development and experiences of a diversifying student population. Patton et al. (2016) specifically highlighted three major critiques: (a) focus on outness as essential in development, (b) lack of generalizability, and (c) the linear nature of previous developmental theories. Outness has been referred to as levels of disclosure for people who hold minoritized sexual and gender identities (Garvey et al., 2018). Garvey et al. (2018) described the historical roots of outness within developmental theories, while noting that the concept emerged from samples normed on White students. They suggest coming out is a highly personal decision and strongly related to students' perceptions of campus climate (Garvey et al., 2018). A related critique of earlier theoretical models is their emergence from studies that did not include representative samples (Bilodeau & Renn, 2005; Patton et al., 2016). As a result, their generalizability to the larger LGBTQ+ population and usefulness for practitioners is limited. Finally, the linear nature of these theories does not account for the varied nature of an individual's experiences (Patton et al., 2016).

Several models have emerged since 2011 and have considerable utility for faculty and staff on college campuses. For example, Dillon et al. (2011) developed the unifying model of sexual identity development, which broke the development of sexual identities—both privileged and minoritized—into several statuses. The "sexual identity statuses" that comprise Dillon et al.'s model begin with Adrienne Rich's (1980) notion of *compulsory heterosexuality* (i.e., the identity most consistent with societal assumptions of straightness). Next, Dillon et al. contest, individuals move to a state of *active exploration*, in which they reflect on and interrogate their sexual/social identities. The individual may enter a state of *diffusion*, characterized as the absence of deliberate reflection on, or commitment to, an identity or identities. They may linger in this diffuse state or bypass it entirely, moving on to *deepening and commitment* to firm sexual and/or social identities. Many people with minoritized sexual identities spend time in the diffusion status, while straight people may move directly from compulsory to committed heterosexuality. Finally, a person may reach *synthesis*, whereupon their individual sexual identity, social identities, and attitudes towards questions of sexual orientation cohere into a holistic "sexual self-concept" (Patton et al., 2016, p. 664). This model has significant application for scholars and practitioners in higher education and student affairs because it affirms that sexual identities need not be defined by the way they adhere to—or deviate from—heterosexist social norms. In other words, sexual identity development happens to everyone, regardless of their particular identities or the ways those might shift over time.

Another example is Vaccaro and colleagues' (2015) minoritized identities of sexuality and gender (MIoSG) students and contexts model. Their model drew from previous scholarship around campus climate, notably Bronfenbrenner's (1993) bioecological model. In their MIoSG Students and Contexts Model, Vaccaro et al. (2015) reaffirmed Bronfenbrenner's position that considerations of institutional context are essential to any understanding of student development in college. The model was set up to reflect the various contexts which might impact the development of students with MIoSG and contribute to a student's "holistic sense of self" (Vaccaro et al. 2015, p. 29). Where previous studies have focused primarily on institutional/campus contexts, Vaccaro et al. also consider sociopolitical contexts, time contexts, and "homeplace" contexts (i.e., a student's relationship to family, peers, spirituality, and employment) to form an understanding of how students with MIoSG make meaning of themselves and the development of their identities (p. 35).

Similarly, Woodford et al. (2016) used Astin's (1977) input-environment-outcome (I-E-O) model to similar ends. They expounded on the relevance of the I-E-O model to LGBTQ+ students, asserting that "although students' inputs directly affect their academic achievement and other outcomes, they are mediated by the college environment" (Woodford et al. 2016, p. 65). In applying Astin's model to LGBTQ+ students, Woodford et al. characterized inputs (i.e., the values, qualities, and experiences that students bring with them to the campus environment) along similar lines to Vaccaro et al.'s (2015) understanding of homeplace contexts. Woodford et al. (2016) categorized these inputs as academic, nonacademic (i.e., home and community contexts), and related to LGBTQ identity and expression. Woodford et al. (2016) also noted that institutional/campus contexts were significant to LGBTQ+ students' likelihood of persisting in higher education. In other words, inclusive or exclusive campus environments have a direct impact on LGBTQ+ students' level of engagement, academic or otherwise.

According to the I-E-O model, Woodford et al. (2016) identified four categories of outcomes for LGBTQ+ students. Their *academic outcomes* are characterized by their persistence in higher education and the knowledge/competence with which they leave an institution. Woodford et al. (2016) also posited that *mental health outcomes* are vital to the development of students with MIoSG (for example, if their campus contexts were rife with heterosexism, their well-being is likely to be affected even after leaving that campus). On a related note, Woodford et al. (2016) asserted that *social/community* aspects of the campus environment impact students with MIoSG's ability to connect with the wider LGBTQ community later in life, as well as influencing their *identity/expression* in and beyond campus contexts.

The consideration of environment is important for faculty and staff, as the conditions created within college departments and classrooms can influence students' identity development. Below, I list several questions for faculty and staff to consider regarding how these models may be applied on college campuses. This list is not exhaustive, but rather a starting place for creating an inclusive and affirming learning environment for LGBTQ+ students.

- To what extent are heterosexist social norms broken or intact on campus?

- How might individual faculty or staff work to deconstruct heterosexist norms on campus?

- Are social norms, including heterosexist norms, discussed in the classroom?

- Do students have an opportunity to reflect on their own social identities in relation to social norms within classroom assignments?

- How can faculty and staff create a welcoming and affirming classroom environment for LGBTQ+ students?

- In their individual interactions with students, how do faculty and staff affirm students' sexual and gender identities?

Barriers to Research on LGBTQ+ College Students

Despite an influx of literature examining the experiences of LGBTQ+ college students since 2010, barriers still impede scholarship on the subject. Further, institutional-level data is often lacking in indicators for minoritized sexual and gender identities. This section highlights barriers for LGBTQ+ research in higher education and student affairs.

Survey Instrument Limitations

Renn and Reason (2013) identified only one generalist higher education survey with sexual identity markers: the Harvard College Alcohol Study. As of 2013, no national surveys included gender identity markers beyond a binary gender construction or, at most, a catch-all "transgender" status marker (Renn & Reason, 2013). More recently, several national, large-scale, generalist surveys have begun to include sexual and gender identity markers. Higher education organizations must include markers for sexual and gender identity on all surveys, so scholars and practitioners can continue to identify areas for improvement and intervention to best serve the growing population of students who hold minoritized sexual and/or gender identities. The absence of these markers, or the common conflation of sex and gender on surveys, may also be a factor in whether an LGBTQ+ student decides to participate in a survey. If students do not see themselves in these surveys, they may be less likely to respond (Bennett, 2019). Despite some advances, both the conflation of sex and gender and the lack of these identifiers limit the ways institutions can use data from these surveys on their campus (Garvey et al., 2019).

Research on LGBTQ+ collegians' academic success has also focused on changing the ways LGBTQ+ students are conceptualized in higher education. Garvey (2017) studied the ascendance of queer as a social identifier, and specifically its use in higher education scholarship. In his article, Garvey draws upon existing work by Dugan and Yurman (2011) to critique the ways LGBTQ+ student populations are homogenized in educational research. Garvey (2017) argues that including queer as an identifier—along with lesbian, gay, and bisexual (LGB)—in survey response options allows for a more diverse range of minoritized sexual identities to be represented in the resultant survey data. Further, Garvey asserts that conceptualizing queerness solely in terms of LGB labels reifies hegemonic understandings of sexual identity development.

These considerations are critical for campus practitioners and administrators, who use such surveys for institutional effectiveness and assessment efforts. While asking relevant and inclusive questions is important, designing a broad set of response items is perhaps more so, as utility of the data varies based on the options students are provided on surveys. Several resources might be helpful in creating survey questions with inclusive gender and sexual identity markers, including:

- ACPA Standards for Demographic Questions (https://www.myacpa.org/sites/default/files/Proposal-Demographic-Questions-and-Responses-2.pdf)

- The Williams Institute Best Practices for Asking Questions to Identify Transgender and Other Gender Minority Respondents on Population-Based Surveys (https://williamsinstitute.law.ucla.edu/wp-content/uploads/geniuss-report-sep-2014.pdf)

- The Williams Institute Best Practices for Asking Questions about Sexual Orientation on Surveys (https://williamsinstitute.law.ucla.edu/wp-content/uploads/SMART-FINAL-Nov-2009.pdf)

Institutional Data Limitations

While large-scale survey instruments have utility for higher education and student affairs researchers and administrators, institutional data do, as well. These data serve a variety of needs on college campuses, including providing a profile of the student population and allowing faculty, staff, and administrators to disaggregate assessment findings by specific student subpopulations as well as to identify areas for improvement. When institutional data do not include markers for sexual and gender identities, however, campus administrators are limited in the analyses they can conduct and interpretations they can infer. For example, if an institution does not accurately include gender within its data system, FYE office staff cannot deduce whether trans students persist to the second year at the same rate as their cisgender peers.

Student records systems at institutions typically are created by an educational organization or are homegrown; systems look differently based on their creator. Examples of institutional data systems created by educational organizations include Ellucian's Banner, PeopleSoft Campus Solutions, and Skyfactor's Mapworks. Homegrown systems can be created by any institution and usually mirror educational organization offerings but are specified to that institution's context.

The Campus Pride Index has self-reported data from colleges and universities that include gender and sexual orientation identity markers in their institutional datasets (Campus Pride,

2018). Of the sample I analyzed, only 92 institutions allowed students to self-report sexual orientation on admissions or post-enrollment forms (Campus Pride, 2018; see Figure 2.2). For reference, this equates to less than 3% of all U.S. postsecondary institutions. Campuses that allow students to report gender identity or expression appear to be similarly low nationally: 132 institutions allowed students to self-report gender identity or expression on such campus forms (Campus Pride, 2018; see Figure 2.3). Further, the CPI data do not detail specifics on the information these institutions collect. It is unclear, for example, whether gender is represented beyond a binary or if sexual identity is an open-ended response.

As seen in Figure 2.2, several states did not have any institutions that reported collecting sexual identity data. Further, the gaps for institutions in the Southeast, Midwest, and central United States are notable. When institutions in these regions did participate in the CPI, they were unlikely to report having sexual identity as a marker on admissions or post-enrollment forms. This may signify some efforts by institutions in these areas toward LGBQ+ inclusion but a lack of specific work in the areas of enrollment management and institutional research.

Patterns of institutional data related to gender identity are similar to those for sexual identity, with slightly more institutions including gender identity as part of admissions and post-enrollment forms. The map of gender identity indicators also shows slightly more geographic diversity among institutions collecting this information than those who reported collecting data on sexual identity. It is important to note, however, that while some regions had more institutions collecting these data, those areas also had numerous institutions not participating in data collection. This suggests that geographic region is not the only limiting factor with respect to inclusive student record systems.

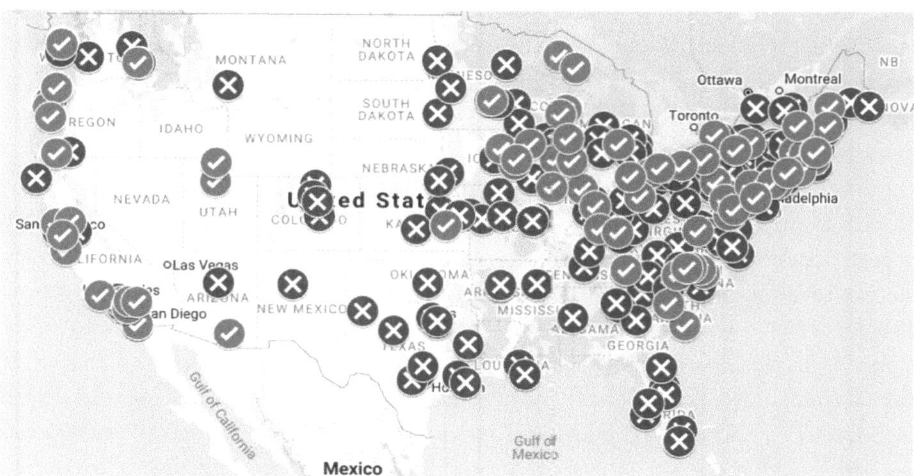

Figure 2.2. Geographic illustration of sexual identity institution-level data by U.S. state. X marks signify campuses that responded to the CPI but did not report having sexual identity institutional-level data. Check marks signify campuses that responded to the CPI and reported having sexual identity institution-level data. Data from Campus Pride (2018). Map figure from Google Maps.

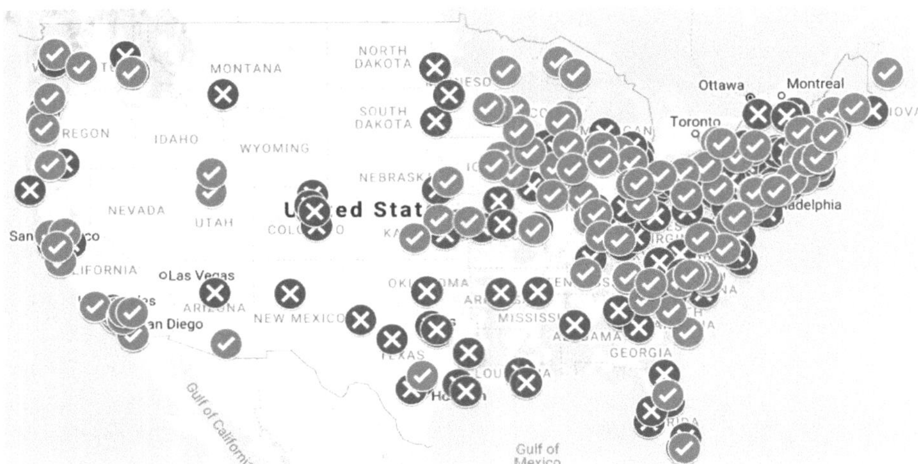

Figure 2.3. Geographic illustration of gender identity institution-level data by U.S. state. X marks signify campuses that responded to the CPI but did not report having gender identity institutional-level data. Check marks signify campuses that responded to the CPI and reported having gender identity institution-level data. Data from Campus Pride (2018). Map figure from Google Maps.

Additionally, the Campus Pride Index hosts the Trans Policy Clearinghouse. Similar to the Index, this Policy Clearinghouse lists institutions who self-reported having specific inclusive measures and practices on campus. According to the Trans Policy Clearinghouse, 260 colleges allow students to use a chosen name on records, 60 colleges allow students to change their gender marker without medical intervention paperwork, and 43 institutions allow students to include their pronouns on course records (Campus Pride, n.d.-c). These practices are ideal for allowing students to accurately represent themselves in their student record, and therefore allowing faculty and staff to have important information like chosen name and pronouns.

The availability of institutional data directly influences the quality of large-scale empirical and campus-based assessments studies of educational outcomes, including persistence and retention. Institutions have more autonomy to adapt their student records systems to include inclusive sexual and gender identity markers, if the system is homegrown. In order to make such changes, information technology (IT) administrators on an individual campus will need to create modules within the student information system to represent the data markers (i.e., sexual identity, gender identity). For institutions that use educational organization systems, such as Ellucian's Banner and PeopleSoft Campus Solutions, updates have been added since 2014 to include more inclusive options. Having inclusive data within the student record system (reported by the student) will not only allow students to "see" themselves within the university record, but also allow university administrators and practitioners to evaluate how LGBTQ+ students are doing compared to their heterosexual and cisgender peers. These findings could lead to intentional interventions related to support for the success of LGBTQ+ students.

Summary and Conclusion

The literature on LGBTQ+ college student populations has blossomed in many ways since 2010. The publications focused on the experiences of LGBTQ+ collegians varied by subject matter, including the three categories that Renn (2010) established and expanding to include two additional topics (i.e., outcomes beyond identity and climate; LGBTQ+ campus education programs). While the findings show progress is far from complete, it is my hope that this book provides the impetus to push higher education toward creating change for affirming and inclusive environments for LGBTQ+ collegians. The individual studies introduced in this chapter will be explored in greater depth as they relate to LGBTQ+ students' transition into (Chapter 3), through (Chapter 4), and out of college (Chapter 5).

Chapter 3

Transitioning Into Collegiate Contexts

The ways that students are socialized into postsecondary contexts influence their likelihood for success. Feldman's (1976) model of socialization includes four components: (a) anticipatory socialization, (b) accommodation, (c) role management, and (d) outcomes. The first of these, anticipatory socialization, is particularly significant for students' transition into college. According to Feldman, anticipatory socialization encompasses all the messages and information a person receives before they enter an organization and whether those messages are congruent upon entry. Within higher education, this would include all of the messages students receive before applying (e.g. campus visits/tours), during their application process, after accepting an offer of admission (e.g., selection of housing), and before they enter the institution (e.g., orientation, registration). The presence of LGBTQ+ students on college campuses has increased significantly over time due to both more entering students being out in their identities and increased awareness through student record systems (Renn & Reason, 2013).

Since 2010, the scholarship on LGBTQ+ students' transition into college has also increased, including explorations of inclusive recruitment and admissions practices, which allow students to disclose their identities while ensuring that student affairs professionals are supportive of these populations both before and after they arrive on campus. There is still much to be done, however, if the diverse needs of entering LGBTQ+ college students are to be fully met within anticipatory and early socialization processes. This chapter outlines the challenges LGBTQ+ college applicants face, recruitment efforts by institutions, the first-year experience for these students, and their adjustment into college.

Challenges for LGBTQ+ Applicants

Baum (2012) used five case studies from his tenure in recruitment at Tufts University in Massachusetts to identify some of the struggles LGBTQ+ college applicants face. In particular, some prospective students' families might not know of or accept their students' sexual or gender identities, making disclosure during the recruitment and application process difficult. Given this challenge, Baum argued that such complications may result in LGBTQ+ students' identities being overlooked by—or withheld from—student affairs professionals, thereby limiting their ability to help these students transition into a collegiate environment.

Newhouse (2013) took up a similar but more focused line of inquiry, investigating the ways higher education institutions recruit and support transgender students. Newhouse argued that institutional administrators may not fully recognize the complexities around trans identities and modes of gender expression, which can lead to less focus on the recruitment and success for trans collegians when they enter and navigate throughout college. She also noted that because many trans individuals come out during adolescence, their early college years are important to their identity development, and the admissions process can potentially set the tone for the rest of their collegiate experience. The conflation of sex and gender on many institutional forms reinforces assumptions that students' gender markers and pronouns always align with those assigned at birth. Such assumptions work to erase and delegitimize the identities of trans and gender-nonconforming (TGNC) collegians, while perpetuating cis-normative conceptualizations of sex and gender as inviolably binary (Beemyn & Brauer, 2015). Further, the lack of inclusive student records can put students at risk. Beemyn and Brauer (2015) stated, "Trans people who are not read as trans and who are not out are at constant risk of having their identity disclosed should their assigned name appear, which makes them targets for discrimination" (p. 480).

Institutions can potentially circumvent some of these challenges by having inclusive forms at all stages of the recruitment, admission, and enrollment process. While all postsecondary institutions receiving Title IX funding must report demographics to the Department of Education through the Integrated Postsecondary Education Data System (IPEDS; National Center for Educational Statistics, n.d.), this report does not include gender or sexual identity. Collecting these data would require additional effort by the institution and is not federally mandated. Having inclusive records, however, allows students to see themselves within the institution. Baum (2012) noted that merely having inclusive options can be a signal to prospective students that the institution values LGBTQ+ students. It also allows faculty and staff to correctly address students, reducing the burden on the student to disclose their name and pronoun (Linley & Kilgo, 2018). Institutions could also use this information to provide specific and targeted recruitment for LGBTQ+ prospective students, ensure current students are aware of available resources, and investigate LGBTQ+ student persistence.

In addition to inclusive admissions applications, institutions should have post-enrollment forms that allow students to edit their demographic data, including sex, gender, name, and pronouns (Linley & Kilgo, 2018). Having the ability to change such markers removes the burden of being out during the admissions process and avoids potential conflicts with parents and family members (Baum, 2012). Linley and Kilgo (2018) specifically focused their work on creating inclusive admissions applications at the University of Iowa that give students the option to edit their name, gender, and pronouns at any time during their enrollment. These forms would need to be separate from the information accessible by guardians under the Family Educational Rights and Privacy Act (FERPA). While this would require more work on the part of the institution, it would allow students to opt to disclose their authentic identities in order to be addressed appropriately and receive relevant resources. For trans students, it would also reduce their risk of being outed and thereby lessen the chance of facing discrimination (Beemyn & Brauer, 2015).

Figure 3.1 highlights data from the Campus Pride Index on opportunities to edit student records at participating institutions. Of the 299 not-for-profit institutions included in my sample, 221 (74%) reported having an easy process for students to change their name in their student records (Campus Pride, 2018). The ability to change their name within student records allows trans students the ability to ensure their name of reference or chosen name is accessible by campus faculty and staff, minimizing the trans student's burden to continually correct their name for faculty and staff when their chosen name does not align with their legal name.

Fewer institutions (n = 170, 57%) reported having simple options for students to change their gender on institutional records. Having gender on institutional records allows students to see themselves within the institution. It also allows college administrators to more accurately track outcomes by gender, which can allow for interventions to increase retention and other outcomes for students on campus.

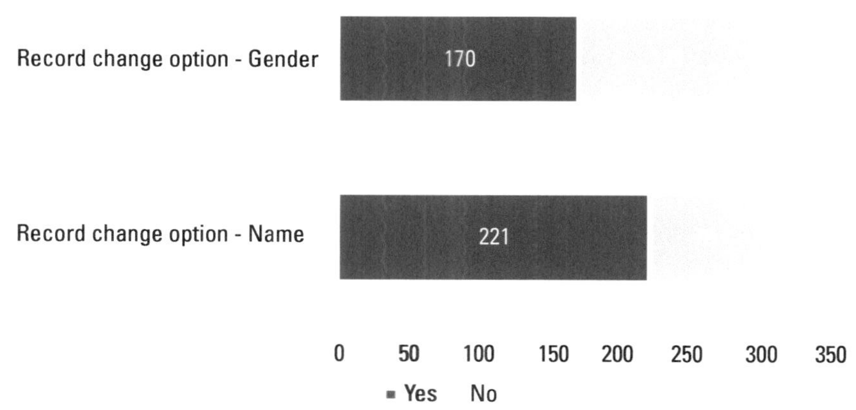

Figure 3.1. Availability of student records change by name and gender (Campus Pride, 2018).

Recruiting Prospective Students from LGBTQ+ Populations

In line with Newhouse's (2013) observations, it is important to remember that the transition into higher education for many prospective students begins in high school. Jackson (2016) posited that support for queer-identified college hopefuls should begin with high school counselors. Jackson undertook a phenomenological study to understand the experiences of LGBTQ+ college students, reflecting on the transition from secondary to tertiary educational contexts. Participants described confronting hostile, unsupportive cocurricular environments and a lack of support in their home lives (Jackson, 2016). These negative events arguably reinforced the participants' perceptions of learning environments as intrinsically queerphobic. Similarly, participants also encountered stumbling blocks in their efforts to self-determine, understand, and develop their own sexual and/or gender identities.

The participants who overcome these struggles, however, also remarked on an enhanced sense of their own empowerment and increased resilience in the face of oppressive or unsympathetic forces in their institutional contexts (Jackson, 2016). Jackson (2016) advocated for better support for LGBTQ+ students by high school counselors as a means of mitigating these negative educational outcomes, as well as fostering empowerment and resilience before and throughout the transition to higher education. Given the wide variance of campus climates that LGBTQ+ high school students face (James et al., 2016; Kosciw et al., 2016), it is perhaps unrealistic to expect all secondary contexts to provide inclusive experiences for queer and trans teenagers prior to college. At the same time, however, this instability in reliable support for high school students places more impetus on higher education to practice inclusive recruitment.

Among the ways colleges and universities can make their admissions practices more queer-friendly is by designing admissions materials to represent more diverse student populations. Gendered language (i.e., "he or she") should be avoided. Yet, Mathis and Tremblay (2010) note the challenges of representing LGBT students visually on such websites, given their historical exclusion from diversification efforts, as well as their status as "invisible" on many campuses (Cegler, 2012, p. 19). The authors argue that queer-identified students must be central to ongoing efforts to diversify admitted student populations, if admissions offices are to be aligned with institutional principles regarding inclusivity (Mathis & Tremblay, 2010). They recommend that admissions offices collaborate with existing campus resources for LGBTQ+ students, such as student organizations and resource centers, and strive for consistent representational practices across institutional websites, social media accounts, and print pieces. Admissions offices that espouse principles of representation, diversity, and inclusion, they contested, would augment efforts to recruit and admit students with minoritized identities of sexuality and gender (Mathis & Tremblay, 2010).

Despite limited research on the targeted recruitment of gay, lesbian, bisexual, and trans (GLBT) students, Cegler (2012) acknowledges that efforts to enroll more GLBT students are ongoing, often spurred by pressure from external advocacy groups. The CPI collects data on inclusive admissions practices, such as participating in LGBTQ+ admissions fairs, offering scholarships specifically for LGBTQ+ students, and facilitating training on LGBTQ+ issues for admissions staff. As highlighted in Figure 3.2, fewer than one third of institutions in the sample (30.43%) reported participating in LGBTQ admissions fairs. A slightly higher percentage of institutions (36.79%) reported offering scholarships for

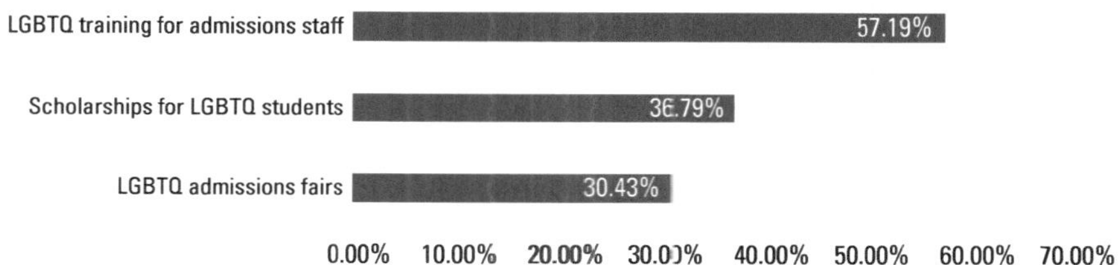

Figure 3.2. Inclusive admissions practices (Campus Pride, 2018). (*N* = 299).

LGBTQ+ students. The highest percentage of institutions (57.19%) reported providing training for admissions counselors (Campus Pride, 2018).

While the presence of inclusive admissions practices is encouraging, Baum (2012) warns they may not be effective in reaching all LBGTQ+ students: "for those students unsure or struggling with their sexuality, college fairs are not how we reach [them]" (p. 28). Instead, Baum suggested institutions make efforts to recruit students in a variety of ways, both through admissions fairs and more subtle efforts, such as college websites with resources for LGBTQ+ students. Institutions should also strive, however, to provide ample training to admissions staff who work with prospective LGBTQ+ applicants.

LGBTQ+ Students and College Adjustment

Acclimation to and integration within the higher education environment is an important task for all entering students. Kirsch et al. (2015) used a matched sample of incoming LGB students and their heterosexual counterparts to determine differences and similarities in these populations' psychosocial adjustment to collegiate living. While both LGB and heterosexual students experienced a significant increase in psychological distress during their first semester, this distress was consistently greater among LGB students. Kirsch et al. noted that the first year of college marks a developmental milestone for many students. To ensure a successful transition for LGB students, institutions must therefore be cognizant of how aspects of transitioning to college can be detrimental to students' psychosocial well-being and their cognitive–affective strengths.

Sense of belonging is an important factor for college students' satisfaction with and desire to stay at an institution (Hurtado & Carter, 1997; Museus, 2014; Strayhorn, 2012). Sense of belonging is also integral to Vaccaro and Newman's (2017) grounded-theory study on first-year lesbian, gay, bisexual, pansexual, and queer (LGBPQ) students' perspectives on their institutional contexts. Vaccaro and Newman offered theoretical propositions contingent on three social structures: the university, social groups, and authentic friendships. Other moderating factors included individuals' degree of outness, their sexual identity development, and the messages advanced by the university with regard to LGBPQ student populations. Vaccaro and Newman developed four major theoretical propositions:

- Pro-LGBPQ messages on campus are vital to students' sense of belonging.

- The time it takes to develop friendship belonging, or belonging based on authentic peer relationships, is more involved than university belonging, or belonging within a university.

- Students' identity development influences their needs for a sense of belonging on campus.

- Students require authentic, rather than casual friendships. (Vaccaro & Newman, 2017)

These findings add nuance to the ways that colleges programmatically foster sense of belonging for LGBPQ collegians. Vaccaro and Newman (2017) recommend several steps for institutions to foster a sense of belonging for LGBPQ students, including affirming messages regarding LGBPQ identities and issues, support structures to foster peer interactions and belonging for LGBPQ students, and professional development for faculty and staff to learn how to facilitate inclusive campus environments for LGBPQ students, among others.

Similarly, Alessi et al. (2017) take a grounded-theory approach to exploring lesbian, gay, bisexual, queer, and questioning (LGBQQ) college students' experience in the first year. The authors recruited 21 LGBQQ students for focus groups and asked them to reflect on their first year in higher education (Alessi et al., 2017). Their findings echoed much of what Kirsch et al. (2015) and Vaccaro and Newman (2017) concluded. Participants discussed the challenges of increased independence, as well as stressors linked specifically to their minoritized identities, such as queerphobic stigma from their peers (Alessi et al., 2017). One important distinction from previous studies, however, is that the authors characterized students' response to minority stress as one of developing resilience. Participants cited social organizations, self-actualization, pride, and supportive cocurricular environments as sources of strength in the face of a challenging transition into collegiate life (Alessi et al., 2017).

Yet environmental factors and microaggressions can undermine sense of belonging for LGBTQ+ students. In an effort to understand the specific challenges faced by trans collegians, Woodford and colleagues (2017) conducted a mixed-methods study on environmental microaggressions, which are contexts at the institution-level, and their influence on well-being and academic development. They surveyed 152 trans students about the environmental challenges of college living (e.g., exclusionary language on forms; lack of access to safe, comfortable living and bathroom facilities) and found that such microaggressions negatively affected trans students' academic outcomes (Woodford et al., 2017). In addition, they interviewed 18 trans students to learn more about systemic challenges to their well-being. Findings from the qualitative portion of their study highlighted barriers associated with access to restrooms, inclusive forms, and gender-inclusive housing options (Woodford et al., 2017). Institutions can work to reduce environmental microaggressions for trans students. For example, Woodford et al. (2017) suggest having inclusive restrooms that are easily accessible, training faculty and staff on trans issues and inclusion, and having practitioners "help trans* collegians to develop a positive self-concept in light of the systemic minority stressors they face in their learning environments" (pp. 108-109). Similarly, Squire and Beck (2016) recommend institutions convert single-user restrooms (i.e., labeled as "women" or "men") into non-gendered spaces. Gendering of single-user restrooms is unnecessary, and relabeling them is a simple way for campuses to promote a more gender-inclusive environment.

Strayhorn and Mullins (2012) adopted minoritized racial and sexual identities as their framework for investigating certain queer-identified student populations. Their inquiry focused specifically on Black gay male undergraduate students' experiences in on-campus housing. The authors interviewed 29 participants who reported a variety of racist, homophobic, and heterosexist encounters, on both interpersonal and systemic levels. Participants described both overt and insidious displays of racism from White peers, as well as homophobia from male peers of their own race (Strayhorn & Mullins, 2012). Perhaps more distressingly, participants cited policies and programs within their residence halls that perpetuated homophobic and heterosexist attitudes. The combination of racist, homophobic, and hegemonic sociocultural forces within their residence halls left these participants feeling increasingly isolated and alienated from their peers.

Orientation

One strategy institutions might adopt to support LGBTQ+ student adjustment to collegiate environments is an FYE program specifically for minoritized populations. Squire and Norris (2014) illuminated the benefits of such a program by giving background on FYE programs in general and on the distinct needs of lesbian, gay, bisexual, transgender, queer, and ally (LGBTQA) students in particular. Squire and Norris described The One Project, an add-on initiative started at the University of Maryland, College Park (UMD), that included summer programming, social events, and even a specialized convocation designed to foster community and a sense of belonging among LGBTQ+ students. At the time of their publication, Squire and Norris noted the success of The One Project, both in terms of programmatic assessment at UMD and on a national level.

Residence Life

Krum et al. (2013) stated that gender-inclusive housing "allows students of different legal sexes to live together in the same residence hall room, suite, or apartment" (p. 65). They described five configurations of gender-inclusive housing:

- students of different sexes living in same room;

- students of any sex living together in an apartment with private bedrooms;

- housing matching based on gender rather than sex;

- a pair of female students and male students each sharing bedrooms, but both pairs sharing common spaces of the apartment; and

- single rooms for trans students (Krum et al., 2013).

Krum and colleagues also highlighted various ways that gender-inclusive housing becomes available to students—whether students must request it, if it is a given within all room assignments, or whether it is available to new and/or returning students. Some of these options place unnecessary burdens on students. For example, one institution required students interested in gender-inclusive housing to attend a group meeting, which may force TGNC students who are not yet out to come out to peers and residence life staff. For trans students who are not out as trans, having to out themselves to peers could be a barrier to seeking gender-inclusive housing. In another example from Krum et al. (2013), one institution allowed first-year students to appeal for an exception to the policy that made gender-inclusive housing only available to returning students. Again, such a policy might mean gender-inclusive housing is out of reach for new students who are not yet out and whose parents or guardians are heavily involved in the admissions process.

Pryor and colleagues (2016) recommended that institutions consider individual students when examining gender-inclusive options, suggesting this as a way to find safe and supportive options for each trans student seeking gender-inclusive housing. They also suggested that residence hall staff receive more education on trans issues to help mitigate some of the burdens placed on students when interacting with staff who may be inadequately trained on LGBTQ+ identities or issues. While it is sometimes common for student leaders and residence life staff to receive training on LGBTQ+ issues, it is important to provide these trainings for all staff, including those who work with assignments and facilities.

According to the CPI (2018), the most common residence life practice was training staff on LGBTQ issues and concerns (89%), followed by gender-inclusive restrooms (69%), gender-inclusive housing options for returning students (67%), gender-inclusive housing options for new students (59%), gender-inclusive shower facilities (56%), roommate matching (51%), and LGBTQ living–learning communities (41%). Mobley and Johnson (2015) found that HBCUs "disregard[ed] the presence of lesbian, gay, bisexual, and transgender

[LGBT] students on their campuses" (p. 80). Yet, my analysis of the CPI data revealed that minority-serving institutions (MSIs) were among those reporting these practices, suggesting the situation may be changing on some, if not all, MSI campuses.

Examples of Inclusive Excellence

The CPI data analyzed throughout this chapter provide a snapshot of what some institutions are doing related to inclusive practices for LGBTQ+ students. Because these data provide limited insight into what inclusion looks like in practice, I highlight two examples of inclusive excellence here: the trans-inclusive admissions application and student records system at the University of Iowa and the gender-inclusive housing and LGBTQ+ first-year learning community at Kennesaw State University.

Iowa's Admissions and Registrar's Office Data System

In 2016, the University of Iowa (UI) revised its admissions applications to decouple sex and gender (Linley & Kilgo, 2018; Trans @ Iowa, n.d.). This change allowed students to report their sex and their gender rather than just their sex, as is typical for student records. Collaborative advocacy work by students, faculty, and staff led UI's administration to reconsider demographic options on admissions applications, ultimately effecting changes to combat the omission of TGNC identities in their record-keeping (Linley & Kilgo, 2018). Further, UI's revised admissions applications and college records protocols enabled students to self-select gender markers and pronouns. Table 3.1 lists the sex and gender options on UI's admissions applications after the change.

Table 3.1

Sex, Gender, and Pronoun Options on Admissions Applications at University of Iowa

Sex	Gender	Pronouns
Male	Agender	He, him, his
Female	Cisgender	She, her, hers
Intersex	Man	They, them, theirs
Prefer not to answer	Non-binary	Ze, hir, hirs
	Woman	Another set of pronouns not listed above
	Another gender not listed above	
	Prefer not to answer	

Note. Students could select all that apply for gender (Trans @ Iowa, n.d.).

The utility of including these identity markers on the admissions application is that the data are reported by students themselves and feed directly into student records, just like other demographic information such as students' race and residency status. Students can also change these records at any time through their MyUI student portal. For TGNC students, actualizing such changes at the record-keeping level allows for a degree of self-determination. It also allows IU to affirm the students' identities and create a vital sense of inclusion and validation, potentially before students have even registered for classes. These practices contribute to a larger movement toward institutional equity for students with diverse identities of sex and gender. Additionally, practical implications for assessment and evaluation within the institution arise when inclusive policies are in effect. In this case, including these demographic options allows UI to examine the persistence and retention of more subpopulations of TGNC students, while also enriching and diversifying the demographic data needed to properly evaluate accessibility and inclusion on campus.

Kennesaw State's Gender-Inclusive Housing and LGBTQ+ First-Year Learning Community

Kennesaw State University (KSU) has developed an expansive, gender-inclusive living–learning community for LGBTQ+ students. KSU's Stonewall Housing is "geared toward students of all sexual orientations, genders, gender identities, and gender expressions who want to live in a community celebrating their various identities and foster understanding, learning, and community" (Kennesaw State, n.d., para. 1). Students who opt to live in Stonewall Housing can also opt in to KSU's LGBTQ+ First-Year Learning Community.

Stonewall Housing, developed as a collaboration between Housing and Residence Life and LGBTQ Programs, allows students to select roommates of any gender, with each student having their own bedroom and private bathroom in an apartment-style residence hall (Kennesaw State, n.d.). Those who also opt into the LGBTQ+ First-Year Learning Community take three common courses, including a first-year seminar. The learning community is focused on LGBT histories and identities and works to connect students with resources available at KSU (Kennesaw State, n.d.).

According to Jessica Duvall, assistant director of Gender and Sexuality Centers and coordinator of the Safe Space Initiative at KSU, students report that "Stonewall [Housing] provides them a sense of comfort and safety. They do not have fears or concerns about how their roommates may react to their LGBTQ identity and/or LGBTQ affirming perspectives" (personal communication, November 8, 2018). Stonewall Housing also encourages students to explore their identities and gain understanding of the complex nature of identity with peers who might hold similar or different identities (Duvall, personal communication, November 8, 2018). Duvall encouraged those working in higher education to build strong relationships with groups on campus with an eye toward instituting change in the area of housing.

Guiding Questions for Practice

Following are guiding questions for higher education faculty and staff to consider as they reflect on practices related to the transition into collegiate environments for LGBTQ+ students at their institution. In Chapter 6, I share strategies to consider for implementing these practices for building consensus for institutional change.

Admissions and Registrar's Offices

- Do admissions applications and enrollment forms decouple sex and gender?

- Do these forms include gender options beyond a binary?

- Do the forms include options for sexual orientation and gender pronouns?

- What scholarships exist specifically for LGBTQ+ students applying to your institution?

- When prospective students attend campus tours, are gender-inclusive restrooms highlighted? Are LGBTQ+ resources on campus highlighted?

- Do students who provide campus tours to prospective students and their families introduce themselves using their pronouns?

- Are pronouns part of admissions office marketing materials that feature student and staff bios?

- Can students easily and without documentation edit their name, gender, and pronouns within institutionally held records, beginning with the admissions application?

Orientation

- Does orientation programming include resources for incoming LGBTQ+ students?

- If programming includes an overnight event, are gender-inclusive housing options available for trans students that are not segregated from the rest of the incoming class?

- Does the orientation student–staff team represent a diverse set of gender and sexual identities?

- If pre-enrollment training is provided for incoming students, are training modules for creating inclusive LGBTQ+ environments (e.g., Safe Zone training) also provided?

- Do orientation staff and guest speakers provide their pronouns when introducing themselves to students and guests?

- Do name tags for incoming students and their family members include space for pronouns?

- If student organizations and groups participate in orientation, are LGBTQ+ student groups involved?

- Does the institution discuss values related to diversity and inclusion during orientation? If so, are LGBTQ+ identities specifically referenced?

- Are students attending orientation aware of where gender-inclusive restrooms are on campus?

- Do orientation staff engage incoming students in dialogue if derogatory or hate language arises during programming?

First-Year Experience

- If the institution has a topical first-year seminar course, does a section focus on LGBTQ+ studies?

- Similarly, if there are identity-based first-year seminars, is there one for LGBTQ+ students?

- Does the residence life department have a living–learning community for LGBTQ+ students? Does the department offer gender-inclusive housing options?

- Is there a mentoring program on campus that pairs first-year LGBTQ+ students with junior and senior LGBTQ+ students to assist with the transition to college?

- What types of student organizations exist for LGBTQ+ students on the campus? Are they accessible for students seeking to get involved in their first semester on campus?

- In what ways does the general education curriculum incorporate coursework and content on LGBTQ+ history, concepts, and contemporary issues?

- What types of early-alert systems exist for LGBTQ+ students within the first year?

Summary and Conclusion

This chapter examined the transition into college for LGBTQ+ students. I highlighted challenges that LGBTQ+ applicants have, ways for colleges to recruit LGBTQ+ students, and the college adjustment for LGBTQ+ students. Two institutions were highlighted for their work on inclusive student records systems and LGBTQ+ residence life programming. The next chapters focus on the college experience for LGBTQ+ students and then their exit from college.

Chapter 4

Interacting in the Classroom and Throughout College

College can be defined by two major components: curricular (classroom) and co-curricular (extracurricular) experiences. When considering LGBTQ+ students and the previously mentioned negative campus climate at many institutions, administrators should realize the role these experiences have in creating or inhibiting inclusive campus environments. While each student creates their own path throughout college, these two roles are solidified as primary aspects of the college experience. Within this chapter, I will highlight the literature on LGBTQ+ college students within curricular and cocurricular contexts. I will also analyze what various institutions are doing through Campus Pride Index data and provide examples of inclusive excellence. The chapter concludes with guiding questions for staff in a variety of functional areas to consider as they create pathways for LGBTQ+ students to thrive throughout college.

LGBTQ+ Students in Curricular Contexts

Since 2010, several significant lines of inquiry have emerged in the scholarship published on LGBTQ+ college students' curricular experiences. Central among these threads are LGBTQ+ students' experiences in the classroom, the growing importance of inclusiveness to curriculum design, and students' interactions with faculty and staff at their institutions. The literature on these topics ranged from case studies of inclusive praxis by instructors, teaching assistants, and student affairs professionals, to exploring student satisfaction with classroom climate and their relationships with authority figures in curricular environments.

Many of these investigations were, by necessity, qualitative in nature, as they focused on recording and analyzing the experiences of LGBTQ+ students, as well as faculty and staff who address issues around queerness in their professional practice. At the same time, several scholars have used quantitative data to suggest specific variables influencing LGBTQ+ students' perception of their campus climate. Tellingly, scholarship on transgender and gender non-binary students has gained visibility since 2010, evincing a move away from literature that lent primacy to lesbian, gay, and bisexual identities, often at the expense of other queer subjectivities.

In the Classroom

Much of the literature published on LGBTQ+ students' curricular experiences since 2010 has closely scrutinized the classroom itself. As the traditional locus of teaching and learning in most collegiate environments, the classroom is the obvious choice for mining data on these experiences. Linley and Nguyen (2015) identify curricular contexts as significant to the LGBTQ+ student experience and note that these are shaped by a number of external and institutional sociocultural factors. They are careful to note that these factors tend to intersect and overlap; that is, the institutional values that affect curricular contexts often reflect larger sociocultural norms.

Linley and Nguyen (2015) found that such institutional values operate at different levels within higher education, influencing mission; campus climate; policies; resources; and faculty, staff, and student populations at institutions. Consequently, they suggest several measures to improve classroom climate for LGBTQ+ students. These include Safe Zone ally training for faculty and staff and promoting inclusive pedagogical praxis, including considerations of multiple held social identities and strategies to normalize chosen name and pronoun usage. Treating LGBTQ+ students as a homogenous group, Linley and Nguyen argue, risks compounding the marginalization of already liminal subgroups, such as transgender students or queer students of color.

Interestingly, recent scholarship has moved from a generalist approach to queer-identified students in curricular contexts, favoring more focused studies on particular student populations and/or pedagogical environments., Using data from Campus Pride's 2010 National College Climate Survey, Garvey and Rankin (2015) analyzed classroom climate for LGBTQ students across a range of gender identities and expressions. They specifically focused on LGBTQ undergraduates and how they perceived their classroom environment. Paying particular attention to students' gender identities and expressions, the researchers found that gender-conforming students reported positive attitudes about their classroom climate more often than their gender-nonconforming peers. Additionally, Garvey and Rankin posited that variables including outness, LGBTQ-inclusive curricular content, support for queer-identified students from the institution, and the availability of and engagement with LGBTQ-focused campus resources significantly affected how respondents perceived their classroom climate.

Pryor (2015) embarked on a similar line of inquiry in a qualitative study of trans-gender students' curricular experiences. He notes that despite increased visibility of trans students at institutions, research on their experiences in the classroom was limited. Pryor coded data from five trans students at a large midwestern public institution to discern four key themes: (a) the coming-out process; (b) students' interactions with faculty and instructors; (c) support, or lack thereof, from instructors and peers; and (d) the impact of institutional and curricular contexts on students' perceptions of their college environment. Within these themes, the students' individual experiences varied. Some participants reported experiences with faculty not using their chosen name or pronouns to the point where they withdrew from the class, while others reported interactions with instructors to be positive. Participants also reported peers serving as both a support system, by correcting pronouns, but also a source of harassment. In regard to course content, participants reported struggling in courses where gender was an integral part of the course (i.e., foreign language) and in fields that were perceived as more conservative (i.e., education; Pryor, 2015). Put simply, every student's experience varies based on their individual social identities and lived experiences. It is important to remember that LGBTQ+ students are not monolithic when creating inclusive practices within the classroom.

Other researchers have focused on LGBTQ+ students in specific curricular contexts. Furrow (2012) conducted a qualitative study on LGBT students' experience in college composition classes. This study differed from others previously discussed not only because it concentrated on one type of classroom environment, but because the author interviewed both students and faculty. In doing so, Furrow explored the college composition classroom as a microcosm of larger curricular contexts. Students' concerns centered on campus safety, curricular content and structure, rapport with faculty, and writing acumen. While many college students grapple with similar issues, students in Furrow's sample specifically noted the constant connection of these concerns with their sexual or gender identity. For example, Furrow described how students struggled to decide when to speak or write about their identities. Faculty, on the other hand, overall purported their role in composition classrooms to support LGBT students. Yet, they also reported conflict between composition pedagogy and how their teaching praxis engaged with minoritized students. For example, faculty struggled to navigate conflicts between peer review workshops, protecting students' privacy, and providing safe spaces for self-expression. Furrow noted that faculty tried to reiterate to students that they are workshopping the paper content, not the author. Yet, if a student in a short story assignment includes a character who holds a similar minoritized identity as they do, what kind of feedback might they receive, and how might they react to it? Furrow specifically recommended that students and faculty discuss these concerns through open communication, identifying who will read assignments (e.g., peers, TA), and building rapport between faculty and students. The data from both student and faculty participants suggest a number of additional recommendations for faculty teaching LGBT students, including educating oneself about queer-specific issues on campus, managing the classroom to create a safe environment for LGBT students, including LGBT content within the curriculum, and providing space for students to share within writing assignments and then affirming their disclosure (Furrow, 2012).

Some of the other scholarship published since 2010 on LGBTQ+ students in the classroom also explored faculty and instructors' perspective with regard to creating and maintaining inclusive curricular environments. Jaekel (2016) examined how novice teaching assistants in writing classes incorporated LGBTQ+ topics into their curricula. The case study approach explored three graduate teaching assistants' pedagogical strategies, paying particular attention to how they navigated issues of queerness and queer identities. The participants identified a range of strategies used to promote LGBTQ+ inclusion in their classes. These included teaching topics that demonstrated awareness of queer identities, addressing current events in class discussion or assignments, and structuring in-class activities to be as inclusive as possible. Surprisingly, none of the participants in the study reported receiving any formal college teaching training.

As the literature suggests, faculty hold importance within students' experiences with and perceptions of climate in curricular contexts (Furrow, 2012; Garvey & Rankin, 2015; Jaekel, 2016; Linley & Nguyen, 2015; Pryor, 2015). Among the students in Furrow's (2012) study,

> Twenty-two student participants had never had an instructor come out [as queer-identifying]. While 13 students said that faculty had no responsibility to come out, 27 thought … doing so would benefit both LGBT and straight students in terms of increasing awareness. (p. 153)

Regardless of whether a faculty member chooses to come out, institutions can take specific steps to foster environments where LGBTQ+ faculty not only feel supported and welcome, but where LGBTQ+ scholarship is valued. Figure 4.1 provides CPI data on institutional commitment within academic life to recruit LGBTQ+ faculty and staff, LGBTQ+ faculty/staff organization presence, and the recruitment of faculty who study LGBTQ+ topics.

As highlighted in Figure 4.1, of the 299 not-for-profit institutions included in the CPI data I examined, 243 (81%) reported having an institutional commitment within academic life to hiring out LGBTQ+ faculty and staff (Campus Pride, 2018). Such commitment within academic life is important for students, as it signals the presence of LGBTQ+ faculty in visible roles on campus (Furrow, 2012; Linley et al., 2016). What is not clear is whether institutions collect gender or sexual identity data for applicants or new employees as a way to demonstrate an active commitment to diverse hiring practices or whether the strategy is a more passive reliance on anti-discrimination clauses including gender and sexual identities. As such, the CPI provides limited insight into how well institutions are actively recruiting LGBTQ+ faculty and staff.

Recruiting LGBTQ+ faculty alone is not sufficient, however. In order to sustain faculty in these roles, support should be offered for LGBTQ+ faculty and those whose research focuses on LGBTQ+ issues. The fact that less than half of institutions reporting to Campus Pride either had an LGBTQ+ faculty/staff organization on campus or recruited faculty

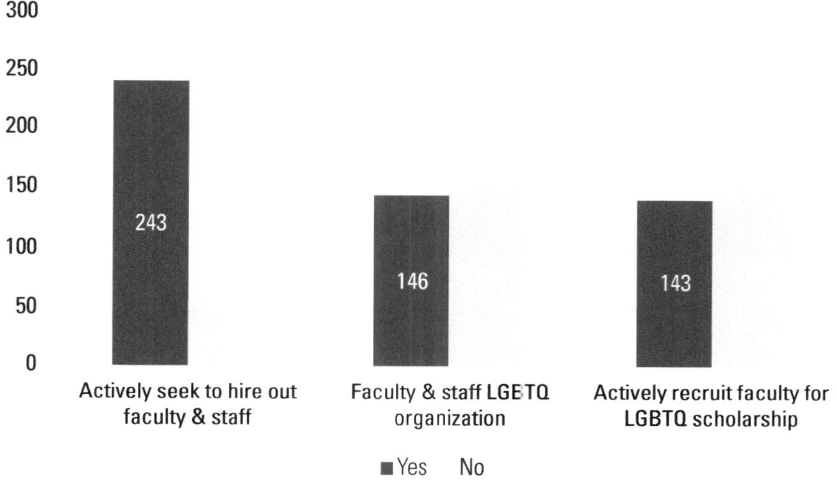

Figure 4.1. Institutional commitment toward LGBTQ+ faculty and staff (Campus Pride, 2018).

for LGBTQ+ scholarship illustrates an overall lack of support for LGBTQ+ faculty and scholarship within curricular contexts. Given the influence that having faculty representation and affirming classroom interactions is for LGBTQ+ students, this is troubling. Institutions should strive to recruit and support LGBTQ+ faculty and scholarship, as these are critical components of the curricular context, including the interactions faculty have with students within and beyond the classroom.

Beyond creating a welcoming and inclusive classroom environment for LGBTQ+ faculty and scholarship, institutions should strive for course offerings that allow for content focusing on LGBTQ+ identities. Of the CPI data that I examined, 261 (87%) institutions reported having LGBTQ+ course offerings and 199 (67%) had a Queer Studies program. While having inclusive and affirming classrooms in general is important for LGBTQ+ students, they should also have opportunities to take classes in which content related to LGBTQ+ identities is present (Furrow, 2012). LGBTQ+ students may exercise caution when discussing or writing about their minoritized gender or sexual identities, but seeing their experiences represented in the curriculum is important to their academic success.

While nearly 90% of institutions that supplied data to the CPI had LGBTQ+ course offerings, we do not have any description of the facilitation of these courses. We cannot glean from the CPI data how many such courses exist, what the course content entails, the frequency of offerings, and how many students are able to enroll. Knowing more about the course design, delivery, and availability of such courses would increase our understanding of how their inclusion in the curriculum impacts the academic climate for LGBTQ+ students.

Interactions With Faculty and Staff

While LGBTQ+ students need support in curricular environments, they can also benefit from positive interactions with faculty and staff outside the classroom. Scholars such as Jaekel (2016) and Ivory (2012) explored instructors' perspectives, but others focused on the relationships between LGBTQ+ students and faculty and staff. Linley et al. (2016) repositioned faculty as a source of support for queer and trans collegians, using qualitative data from a nationwide study of LGBTQ+ student success. To accurately understand those interactions, Linley et al. (2016) investigated faculty and staff interactions with queer and trans students in both formal and informal contexts. In formal classroom exchanges with faculty, LGBTQ+ students expressed feeling supported by certain behaviors, including the use of inclusive language and pronouns by faculty, as well as confronting queerphobic behavior in the classroom. In out-of-classroom contexts, students said they felt supported when faculty and staff participated in events on campus that increased LGBTQ+ visibility or made concerted efforts to promote inclusivity. Students also expressed gratitude for faculty and staff who took on mentoring roles beyond the limits of their job description, particularly when those faculty and staff also openly identified as LGBTQ+ (Linley et al., 2016).

Garvey and Inkelas (2012) pursued a similar line of inquiry; however, they narrowed their focus to include only faculty/staff interactions with lesbian, gay, and bisexual students. They highlighted the dearth of scholarship on the external factors that influence LGB student satisfaction and success and sought to identify the relationship between LGB students and their satisfaction with faculty/staff interactions. Their study found positive predictors for satisfaction related to the college experience, including interacting with faculty on course content and mentorship relationships with faculty. Additionally, Garvey and Inkelas showed LGB students reporting markedly higher satisfaction with faculty/staff interactions than their heterosexual peers. In particular, Garvey and Inkelas observed greater satisfaction with faculty/staff interactions among bisexual students, citing their position as both benefiting and suffering from the effects of heteronormative social structures in collegiate environments. The increased satisfaction is promising, but faculty hold responsibility for educating themselves on LGBTQ+ issues and strategies for creating in- and out-of-class environments.

Of the CPI sample I analyzed, around 150 institutions reported offering training to faculty on issues of sexual orientation and gender identity (Campus Pride, 2018). While the CPI does not report what such training consists of, faculty's awareness and understanding of LGBTQ+ issues does influence students' experiences (Linley et al., 2016). Linley et al. (2016) reported that "training could help faculty learn more about experiences of their LGBTQ students and continue to publicly support them as advisors, instructors, and mentors" (p. 60). For example, such training could help faculty understand the importance of using students' pronouns correctly and provide space for them to practice doing so, as well as educating faculty on campus resources for LGBTQ+ students. Training cannot merely be a check-off box for institutions; instead, it should provide tangible strategies for faculty to use within their classrooms to support and affirm LGBTQ+ students.

LGBTQ+ Collegians in Cocurricular Contexts

As noted earlier, the college experience is split between curricular and cocurricular engagement. LGBTQ+ students, not unlike other college students, are engaged in cocurricular activities and experiences. Given the negative campus climate that exists (Renn, 2010), LGBTQ+ students face additional barriers to, and have unique experiences with, engagement outside the classroom.

Structural Barriers for Engagement

The negative campus climate has encouraged researchers to explore the ways heterosexism, homophobia, and transphobia influence students' experience on campus. Woodford, Kulick, et al. (2014) investigated the role of contemporary heterosexism, which they defined as both overt and subtle discrimination, on LGBQ students' psychological distress. Their study suggested that LGBQ students who reported higher levels of heterosexism had greater levels of psychological distress and lower levels of self-acceptance (Woodford, Kulick et al., 2014). The findings are not necessarily surprising given the previous literature detailing the hostile campus climate for LGBTQ+ students, but they do call into question the influence of such a climate on students' involvement in activities outside the classroom. In particular, it raises questions regarding the structural influence of campus on LGBTQ+ students' ability to become engaged.

One example of this is Worthen's (2014) examination of student athletes and Greek-affiliated students. Worthen noted previous research suggesting that these two student populations and their functional areas (athletics and fraternity/sorority life) might be "easy targets" to espouse negative attitudes toward queer and trans students. Findings from Worthen's study suggested these negative attitudes are much more complex than a blanket covering of blame (Worthen, 2014, p. 169). In particular, Worthen found that several factors, including religiosity and affiliations with LGBT people, mediated some of the negative attitudes of athletes and Greek members.

While Worthen investigated the attitudes of fraternity and sorority members toward LGBTQ+ students, institutions can promote inclusive Greek organizations to support students and create a more affirming campus environment. Yet, very few institutions in the CPI sample I studied reported having an LGBTQ+ specific fraternity or sorority (Campus Pride, 2018).

Institutional type may be a barrier to making resources and cocurricular opportunities available to LGBTQ+ students. McEntarfer (2011) examined the formation of gay–straight alliances at religiously affiliated institutions and noted the need for such alliances as a support system for students in institutions where their identities may clash. Yet, at one institution, the administration denied students' original request for a gay–straight alliance to be formed.

Dirks (2016) examined the influence of language and discourse within university policies on trans students. Dirks explored descriptions of trans students and other trans people on campus, finding that such descriptions might counteract policies enacted to promote trans inclusivity. Both of these studies illustrate that LGBTQ+ students' ability to become engaged in cocurricular activities may not be as simple as one might think. In fact, Zamani-Gallaher and Choudhuri's (2016) examination of the experiences of LGBTQ students in community colleges found students who were being silenced and ignored within the campus climate. One participant reported, "I really don't have nothing to say … except that we were being ignored" (p. 53). If inclusive environments are not present, LGBTQ+ students may not engage in cocurricular activities.

Role of Identity on Cocurricular Experiences

Several scholars have explored the role of LGBTQ+ students' identities on their engagement in cocurricular experiences. Tillapaugh (2015) examined the role of students' identity in his study of cisgender males holding minoritized sexual identities. Specifically, he explored how these participants made meaning of their multiple identities. One major finding was that student leadership roles factored into participants' meaning making, with an important caveat: These roles were not necessarily LGBTQ+ specific. Tillapaugh stated, "Administrators … might work in collaboration with students to find ways that they may want to become engaged and not necessarily attempt to foist LGBT involvement activities upon them" (p. 73). This finding suggests that institutions should strive for opportunities for LGBTQ+ students' engagement beyond those designated solely for them.

One example of this is engagement in high-impact educational practices. Kilgo and colleagues (2019) investigated the role of identity and environment on LGBQ+ students' participation in five high-impact educational practices. Specifically, they examined the role of undergraduate research, internships, academic learning communities, senior capstone experiences, and study abroad on LGBQ+ students' academic development (using a self-report measure of intellectual challenge and growth). Their study found that undergraduate research was a significant predictor for LGBQ+ students' academic development, but that effect is mediated by instructor relations. In other words, student–faculty interactions accounted for a portion (nearly a third in this study) of the relationship between undergraduate research and academic development for LGBQ+ students. This suggests that the facilitation of high-impact practices is critical for LGBQ+ students' academic outcomes.

Carter (2013) examined gay Black students' experiences with collegiate marching bands at HBCUs. Several themes emerged, including negotiating the discourse of the "strong"

African American male, discourse of deficiency and rejection, discourse of passing (being assumed heterosexual), the myth of a singular coming out, coping strategies, the role of family and church, and the significance of being a member of an HBCU marching band (p. 37). These findings permeated decisions that participants made, from choosing a college to how they navigated their band experience—including the instrument they chose to play—to their relationships with their peers after coming out.

To the extent that official and informal online communities constitute part of the cocurricular environment for all students, understanding how LGBTQ+ students navigate those spaces is important. Miller (2017) examined social media use by students who hold both queer and disability identities. His study suggested that students seek online communities for a variety of reasons, including identity exploration and affirmation, as well as involvement (Miller, 2017). Miller stated, however, that online participation did not necessarily prevent offline engagement. The level of engagement that students are seeking online, however, could signify that perceptions of on-campus environments warrant further investigation, particularly for students who hold multiple minoritized identities.

Resources for LGBTQ+ Students

Resource centers, identity-specific student organizations, and social programming for LGBTQ+ students were uniformly represented within the CPI data I analyzed (see Figure 4.2). More than 250 institutions reported having an LGBTQ+ resource center, an LGBTQ+ student organization, or social programming specific to the LGBTQ+ student population (Campus Pride, 2018). Even when resources are available, the literature suggests institutions might not be adequately serving LGBTQ+ students within population-specific services, such as LGBTQ resource centers (Marine & Nicolazzo, 2014), or even through more generalized services on campus, such as health and wellness programs, spiritual resources, and sexual violence services, among others (Manning et al., 2012; Rockenbach et al., 2017; Schulze & Perkins, 2017). For example, Marine and Nicolazzo (2014) examined

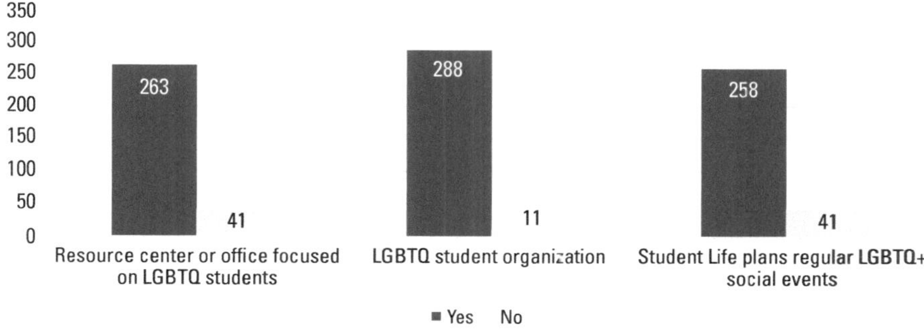

Figure 4.2. Availability of specific resources for LGBTQ+ students (Campus Pride, 2018).

the tensions between LGBTQ resource centers and trans inclusion in the areas of resource center communications, staff, engagement in activism, and programming efforts specific to the trans student population (Marine & Nicolazzo, 2014). They recommend several considerations, including being intentional in the naming of such centers, avoiding the conflation of sexual and gender identities, and hiring trans people.

Johnson and colleagues (2013) suggested that ally training programs, which can be associated with LGBTQ resource centers, often reduce risk factors for suicide within the LGBTQ+ college student population. One example of this is the day-long Safe Zone Program at the University of North Carolina at Greensboro (Johnson et al., 2013). The CPI includes data on safe zone training programs. Of the institutions I examined, almost 90% had such a training program (Campus Pride, 2018). While this is promising, the data offer no insight into how these programs are facilitated.

Beyond ally training, however, which may have an indirect effect on LGBTQ+ students, institutions also need to ensure that services and resources designed for all students are inclusive of LGBTQ+ populations. For example, options for students to report bias incidents and resources for survivors of sexual violence are prevalent on college campuses. Specifically, 94% of institutions participating in the CPI reported having support resources for survivors of sexual violence. Further, 91% reported making bias reporting available to LGBTQ+ students. (The high response rate may be due to federally mandated reporting policies [e.g., Title IX]). The CPI does not provide information on the type of resources and support available to students, limiting the usefulness of these data. Despite the widespread availability of these resources, Schulze and Perkins (2017) found that LGBQ students' awareness of services for survivors of sexual assault was lacking. Indeed, they noted "the potential existence of a systemic problem that prevents sexual minority students who experience a sexual victimization from receiving formal assistance" (Schulze & Perkins, 2017, p. 156). Institutions may need to examine the extent to which the wording of policies or reporting procedures may be excluding LGBTQ+ from official reporting channels—or giving the appearance that they are excluded.

Of the sample of CPI data I analyzed, 202 institutions reported having a counseling/support group for LGBTQ+ students (Campus Pride, 2018). Given the literature espousing the necessity of mental health support for queer and trans populations, all institutions should strive to offer support groups in which students can voice concerns and share experiences in a safe, confidential, and non-judgmental space. In order for LGBTQ+ students to access mental health resources, however, they must have adequate health insurance. Fewer institutions (160) reported covering trans counseling within student health insurance policies, while 133 reported covering health insurance for hormone therapy (Campus Pride, 2018). Ultimately, while LGBTQ+ specific programming and resources often reside within stand-alone resource centers, the burden of educating and providing resources should be shared within the institution.

Examples of Inclusive Excellence

Within this section are two qualitative descriptions of inclusive practices for LGBTQ+ students related to their experiences throughout college: the LGBTQ Campus Ministry Retreat at the University of Notre Dame and the LGBTA Resource Center at North Carolina Central University.

Notre Dame's LGBTQ Campus Ministry Retreat

Students at the University of Notre Dame, Holy Cross College, and Saint Mary's College (both at Notre Dame) can take part in an LGBTQ retreat (University of Notre Dame, n.d.), a collaboration of the Campus Ministry and the Gender Relations Center. It is open to both Catholic and non-Catholic students. In a 2018 article in *The Observer* (a student-run newspaper of Notre Dame and Saint Mary's), the Rev. Joe Corpora said that the goal of the program is for "students [to] leave the retreat being more convinced of God's merciful love no matter what" (Smith, 2018, para. 3). In the same article, Smith (2018) noted that the idea for this type of retreat came more than 20 years earlier. Despite negative press about the event, Notre Dame's Campus Ministry has continued to offer the program for LGBTQ+ students to explore their faith with others on campus who share similar gender and sexual identities.

According to Corpora, working with students on their religious journey is a major resource Campus Ministry provides the LGBTQ+ community (personal communication, November 3, 2018). Corpora said the ministry staff "hope to assist students in thinking through the intersection of faith and sexuality" and "offer an LGBTQ+ faith-sharing group that gathers once a month as well as a once-a-year retreat for LGBTQ+ students." Corpora also pointed to the university's *Beloved Friends and Allies: A Pastoral Plan for the Support and Holistic Development of GLBTQ and Heterosexual Students at the University of Notre Dame* document (available at https://friendsandallies.nd.edu) and noted how this document—assigning value to all of the university's students—aligns well with efforts to minister to LGBTQ+ students (personal communication, November 3, 2018).

North Carolina Central's LGBTA Resource Center

In 2016, North Carolina Central University (NCCU) was noted as the only HBCU with a full-time staff and LGBT space (Consortium of Higher Education LGBT Resource Professionals, 2016). The Lesbian, Gay, Bisexual, Transgender, and Ally (LGBTA) Resource Center at NCCU serves as a model for institutions, specifically MSIs, looking to provide full-time staff and resource support for LGBTQ+ students. The Resource Center provides Safe Zone Ally training, campus programming, a supportive campus space, and a peer leadership program (NCCU, n.d.).

Guiding Questions for Practice

Below are guiding questions for higher education faculty and staff to consider as they reflect on practices related to the collegiate experience for LGBTQ+ students.

Classroom Engagement

- Are LGBTQ+ topics and issues included within the curriculum?

- Do instructors include their own pronouns as part of their syllabus and highlight the importance of using pronouns correctly in managing class discussions?

- How are issues of LGBTQ+ bias and derogatory language handled within the classroom setting?

- Do instructors avoid gendered activities?

- Do instructors evaluate their required readings to ensure LGBTQ+ authors are included?

- Does the center for teaching excellence offer training on creating classroom environments that are safe for LGBTQ+ and other students with minoritized identities?

- Are sample statements related to pronouns and names made available for faculty to incorporate into their syllabi and courses?

- Do instructors receive chosen names and pronouns for students on course rosters?

Student Leadership Involvement

- Does the institution have an LGBTQ+ student organization?

- Are there student organizations for LGBTQ+ students with multiple minoritized identities (e.g., QTPOC students)?

- Does the institution's leadership program provide social justice-oriented programming, including support for LGBTQ+ students?

- Are campus resources across functional areas (not solely within LGBTQ+ or diversity resource centers) facilitated in an inclusive and affirming way?

- What funding structures are in place for LGBTQ+ student organizations in comparison to other non-LGBTQ+ specific organizations?

- Are student leaders at the campus required to participate in LGBTQ+ ally training?

- Are LGBTQ+ students recruited to a broad range of campus leadership roles (e.g., orientation team, residence life, campus tour guides, student government)?

Campus Ministry and Religious Involvement

- What is the climate for LGBTQ+ students within religious settings on campus?

- Are there opportunities for LGBTQ+ students to engage with one another regarding their religious and spiritual development?

- How are campuswide dialogues related to the intersections of gender, sexuality, and religion fostered?

- What response mechanisms are in place for students who use religion as a justification for discrimination, harassment, or exclusion?

Intramural and Recreation Involvement[5]

- Does the institution have policies that regulate trans student placement on to gender-specific intramural and athletic teams?

- What policies are in place for trans and gender-nonconforming students who attend recreation facilities on campus (e.g., restrooms, locker rooms)?

- How does the institution foster a safe and affirming environment for LGBTQ+ athletes at all levels?

- Are coaching and athletic training staff members trained on how to support LGBTQ+ students?

---

[5]Campus Pride has added a Campus Pride Sports Index, accessible at https://www.campusprideindex.org/sports, that may be helpful in considering inclusive practices for intramural sports and recreational activities.

Summary and Conclusion

In this chapter, I highlighted the experiences within college for LGBTQ+ students. This included both curricular and cocurricular activities. The role of climate and environment both inside and outside the classroom is a constant consideration for queer and trans students. Institutions should strive to create welcoming and affirming spaces for LGBTQ+ students, regardless of functional area. In Chapter 5, I highlight LGBTQ+ students' transition out of college, followed by Chapter 6 with practical recommendations for creating institutional change on college campuses for queer and trans inclusion.

Chapter 5

Exiting Collegiate Environments

Colleges and universities have increased their awareness of LGBTQ+ students' distinct curricular and cocurricular needs and have begun to investigate the factors that influence student success among these minoritized populations. Scrutiny of LGBTQ+ students' academic success, in turn, lends itself to the study of LGBTQ+ alumni, especially in terms of their career development and ongoing relationships—or lack thereof—with their higher education institutions. Since 2010, research on the curricular and cocurricular outcomes of LGBTQ+ college students, particularly as they relate to retention, persistence, and engagement as alumni, has developed to reflect growing institutional attention to these student populations. This chapter highlights the literature on collegiate outcomes for LGBTQ+ students and the engagement of LGBTQ+ alumni. Further, data are provided on what colleges are doing to support LGBTQ+ students as they exit collegiate environments, as are guiding questions for how specific areas at institutions can support this population.

LGBTQ+ Collegiate Outcomes

The steady rise in attention to the distinct needs of LGBTQ+ students has led to greater scholarly concern over educational attainment by members of these student populations. Fine (2015) made particular observations about the academic performance of students with minoritized sexual and gender identities in light of previous research on college women and LGB-identified collegians. While prior scholarship indicated that women had higher educational attainment than men (Buchmann & DiPrete, 2006), Fine (2015) found that the "female advantage" and the "LGB bonus" do not apply in combination. In other words, LGB women in bachelor's degree programs deviate from the previously identified trend of higher degree attainment. Further, women who hold minoritized sexual identities, as a whole, are the demographic least likely to graduate college (Fine, 2015).

As noted in Chapter 2, the lack of data on LGBTQ+ students from national survey instruments, many of which are used to assess collegiate outcomes, is a barrier to institutions' understanding of how they are preparing these student populations for life after graduation. Sanlo and Espinoza (2012) call for more research on outcomes for LGBTQ+ collegians, especially those studying at community colleges, a vastly understudied institutional context. The authors recognized the status of these students as "invisible minorities" whose college experiences have often been expressed only anecdotally (Sanlo & Espinoza, 2012). Legg and colleagues (2020) described LGBT students as "one of the most vulnerable populations on college campuses," while pointing out that little information is known about retention rates for these students. Institutional data holders should strive to collect more inclusive student records, including expansive demographic data, to more easily evaluate LGBTQ+ students' success. One emergent model examines queer and trans student success at HBCUs. Mobley and Hall (2020) proposed the "Queer and Trans* HBCU Student Engagement and Retention Practice Model" (p. 507), which focuses on four major areas of queer and trans inclusion: enrollment management, curricular, cocurricular, and alumni engagement. Their model serves as a road map of possibilities in retaining queer and trans students at HBCUs.

In addition to college completion, institutions and other stakeholders are deeply invested in job placement rates among recent college graduates. Schmidt and colleagues (2011) studied the career development of LGBT students, aiming to understand how perceptions of discrimination and support by their institutions guided students' paths into the workforce. Schmidt et al. (2011) found that these perceptions had an observable impact on LGBT undergraduates' adjustment to higher education, as well as their professional decision-making processes. They recommended that career counselors and student affairs professionals be cognizant of students' identities when advising or working with LGBT undergraduate populations. They also argued that, despite existing scholarly attention to contextual factors influencing career development, the manner in which holding LGBT identities affects such development remains understudied.

Of the data I reviewed from the CPI, 186 institutions reported offering LGBTQ+ inclusive career services (Campus Pride, 2018). While our understanding of inclusive career services from these data are limited, Schmidt et al.'s (2011) study emphasized the need for career counselors working with LGBTQ+ students to focus on both the challenges LGBTQ+ students might face, specifically the perceptions of discrimination, and the resilience they hold.

Institutions can easily add resources to pre-existing career services offices to assist LGBTQ+ students in their development. These resources need not be expensive. For example, institutions could offer specific programming allowing LGBTQ+ students to interact with LGBTQ+ people within various career fields. Career services offices could also collaborate with LGBTQ+ focused academic organizations to provide additional resources to students seeking employment. Such resources include national organizations like Out in Science, Technology, Engineering, and Mathematics (oSTEM; see https://www.ostem.org) and institution-specific organizations, such as Reaching OUT in Business within the University of Iowa's Tippie College of Business (see https://tippie.uiowa.edu/student-organizations/reaching-out-in-business).

LGBTQ+ Alumnx

Once LGBTQ+ students' graduate college, their engagement shifts as alumnx. Research has examined how student perceptions of campus climate have changed in recent years (Garvey, Sanders et al., 2017) and gauged philanthropic engagement of LGBTQ+ alumnx with their undergraduate institutions (Garvey & Drezner, 2013).

Using data from the National LGBT Alumni Survey, Garvey, Sanders et al. (2017) compared perceptions of campus climate across generations of LGBTQ undergrads, specifically those who graduated from 1944 to 2013. The results, theoretically undergirded by Renn and Arnold's (2003) reconceptualized ecological model, indicated a shift in perception of campus climate across generations, with more recent LGBTQ graduates taking a brighter view of campus climate. A number of variables, including academic experiences, co-curricular contexts, and differences in institutional and sociocultural values, influenced these findings.

Garvey and Drezner (2013) recommend adopting inclusive practices among advancement staff, such as not assuming alumni are in heterosexual relationships and recognizing gay couples with joint memberships, which were important factors for LGBTQ alumni. The work at UMass-Amherst to update names and honorifics, discussed later in the chapter, is an example of what Garvey and Drezner (2013) referred to as "culturally sensitive" practices of importance (p. 200). These practices could allow students to maintain a sense of institutional commitment to their identity long past their enrollment.

Another way to improve alumni perceptions of their alma maters is by celebrating their academic successes in more individualized ways, such as a specialized commencement ceremony, often referred to as a "lavender graduation." These events typically occur in addition to university-wide ceremonies that all students are invited to attend. According to the Human Rights Campaign (n.d.), the first Lavender Graduation Ceremony occurred at the University of Michigan in 1995 and was created by Dr. Ronni Sanlo. The Human Rights Campaign also highlights that these ceremonies seek to celebrate achievements of LGBTQ students and "provide a sense of community for minority students who often experience tremendous culture shock at their impersonalized institutions" (para. 2). According to the CPI data I analyzed, 196 institutions reported holding a commencement ceremony specifically for LGBTQ+ graduates (Campus Pride, 2018). A graduation ceremony that celebrates the accomplishments of LGBTQ+ students might enhance sense of belonging and connection for LGBTQ+ students to their institutions. As such, they are a relatively simple way to honor students who may have experienced silencing and invisibility in many realms of campus life.

Garvey and Drezner (2013) analyzed philanthropic gestures by LGBTQ alumni and their impact on LGBTQ communities and individuals at their institutions. The authors used data from focus groups made up of LGBTQ advancement staff and alumni advocates from three higher education organizations. They examined how alumni volunteering deepens engagement and encourages similar philanthropic work among LGBTQ communities on campus. Garvey and Drezner recommended that institutions both hire LGBTQ staff and have a positive and affirming advancement office climate.

Hiring staff with diverse sexual/gender identities is a reasonably straightforward institutional strategy for supporting the needs of LGBTQ+ students and alumnx. As noted in Chapter 4, more than 80% (n = 243) of institutions in the CPI sample I analyzed reported having practices in place to hire faculty and staff who hold diverse sexual and gender identities. Garvey and Drezner (2013) suggested, LGBTQ staff "bring with them unique and advantageous networks of potential donors" (p. 212). This is important, as a more diverse staff might provide more opportunities for alumni engagement. Research suggests the presence and needs of LGBTQ+ alumnx, but analysis of CPI data revealed that about one third of institutions (n = 103) have an LGBTQ+ specific alumni group (Campus Pride, 2018).

Examples of Inclusive Excellence

Real-life, descriptive examples of institutions that provide inclusive practices to LGBTQ+ students on campus include the Career Center at Lewis & Clark College and the University of Massachusetts-Amherst (UMass-Amherst), the latter of which gives students options to change their diploma and alumni correspondence name.

Lewis & Clark's Career Center

Lewis & Clark College, in Portland, Oregon, offers online and in-person resources for LGBTQ+ students within its Career Center (Lewis & Clark, n.d.). The online resources relate to coming out within employment settings, the legality of interview questions, traveling concerns for trans job applicants who may have government identification cards with incorrect name or gender listed, LGBTQ+ specific academic and career resources and organizations, and internship opportunities (Lewis & Clark, n.d.). These online resources also provide help for overcoming barriers specific to intersecting identities, such as minoritized gender or sexual identities alongside minoritized racial identities. Additionally, the college offers in-person career counseling to help LGBTQ+ students prepare for the job search.

UMass-Amherst's Diploma and Alumni Correspondence

The Stonewall Center at UMass-Amherst was created in 1985 after anti-LGB incidents on campus (G. Beemyn, personal communication, November 2, 2018). Director Genny Beemyn said the Stonewall Center has been the lead advocate in getting the university to make trans-supportive policy changes over the past decade, including adding "gender identity and expression" to the university's nondiscrimination policy, converting almost all single-user restrooms into gender-inclusive ones, requiring gender-inclusive restrooms in all new construction, creating gender-inclusive housing, having hormones and surgeries for transitioning students covered under student health insurance, having a doctor at the health center who can prescribe and monitor hormones, enabling trans students to have a chosen name on almost all non-legal records and documents, having pronouns on course rosters and in administrative systems, developing a trans-supportive athletic policy, and asking gender identity (and sexual orientation) on the university's admissions form. (personal communication, November 2, 2018)

Of the many resources noted through the Stonewall Center's website, the Office of the University Registrar allows students to update the name on their diplomas (Office of the University Registrar, n.d.), and UMass-Amherst also allows alumni to edit their name and honorific for accuracy in communication with the institution (UMass Trans FAQ, n.d.). In order to update their name on their diplomas, students must provide a written request but are not required to provide legal documentation (Office of the University Registrar, n.d.).

Guiding Questions for Practice

Following are guiding questions for higher education faculty and staff to consider as they reflect on practices related to LGBTQ+ students' transition into collegiate environments.

Career Services

- Does the career services office provide LGBTQ+ students with resources specific to minoritized gender and sexual identities?

- How does the institution work to actively create internship opportunities for LGBTQ+ students, given discriminatory hiring practices elsewhere?

- Does career services collect data on internship and job placement rates, salary, among other outcomes for LGBTQ+ college students?

- Does staff include a full-time employee with a primary responsibility to assist LGBTQ+ students?

- What types of professional development do the staff participate in related to the career development needs of the LGBTQ+ community?

Retention and Outcomes Assessment

* What retention efforts are in place for LGBTQ+ students on campus?

* Are retention and graduation rates tracked by gender identity and sexual orientation?

* What specific issues are raised as concerns by LGBTQ+ students in exit interviews or graduation surveys?

* Do retention staff have data on LGBTQ+ students' experiences on campus in order to track retention?

* Are the experiences of LGBTQ+ students evaluated over the entire collegiate experience?

* How are LGBTQ+ students' development and growth measured throughout college compared to their heterosexual and cisgender peers?

Alumnx and Philanthropic Engagement

* Does the institution have an alumnx group for LGBTQ+ students? If so, how is the group advertised, marketed, and supported by the institution?

* Does the office of alumnx affairs follow up with graduates to share news about LGBTQ+ inclusive practices and resources on the campus?

* What does alumnx outreach look like for graduates who may not have been publicly out during college?

* Are advancement or development staff members trained on how to interact with LGBTQ+ alumnx (formally and informally)?

* What inclusive practices might be enacted related to the use of honorifics, names, and pronouns within alumnx outreach?

Summary and Conclusion

In this chapter, I highlighted collegiate outcomes and alumnx engagement, as major components of LGBTQ+ students' transition out of college. While limited research exists on the retention of LGBTQ+ students, faculty and staff can work towards creating classroom and campus environments that are welcoming, affirming, and supportive to LGBTQ+ college students. In the next chapter, I discuss the tangible ways that faculty and staff can implement practices and strategies to support LGBTQ+ students as they move into, through, and out of college by transforming collegiate environments.

Chapter 6

Concluding Thoughts for Creating Change

This book provides an overview of the literature and practice of higher education and student affairs since Renn's (2010) article "LGBT and Queer Research in Higher Education: The State and Status of the Field." I added two themes—outcomes and LGBTQ+ educational efforts—to the three major themes Renn identified in the literature: visibility, campus climate, and identity and experience. My evaluation of the scholarship since Renn's (2010) call for future research illustrates an increase in studies and a broader set of research questions, but limitations persist. In particular, national, large-scale surveys have been slow to include minoritized gender and sexual identities, as have institutional surveys. Until scholars and institutional administrators collect demographic data that captures queer and trans identities, our understanding of the ways LGBTQ+ students experience postsecondary settings will remain incomplete.

Since 2010, the literature detailing the experiences and development of LGBTQ+ students has examined students' entrance into postsecondary settings, including the challenges these populations face within the admissions process, the efforts of campus administrators to recruit LGBTQ+ students, the first-year experience for these students, and their overall adjustment into college. The bulk of the emergent literature includes studies exploring LGBTQ+ students' experiences and challenges once they arrive on campus. This book highlights both curricular (i.e., classroom environments and interactions LGBTQ+ students have with faculty and staff outside of class) and cocurricular experiences (e.g., the ways such students' multiple identities influence their engagement on campus and resources for LGBTQ+ students in particular). Finally, the book highlights the existing literature on LGBTQ+ students' exit from postsecondary contexts, including college outcomes and the engagement of LGBTQ+ alumni.

Limitations to scholarship on LGBTQ+ populations aside, those who work on college campuses can take tangible steps to move forward to better engage and support this population. Throughout the book, guiding questions have prompted examination of practices and made recommendations for action across a variety of postsecondary functional areas. When considering these questions and recommendations for action, I implore all college faculty and staff to consider tangible ways that they can create change in their own practice or on the larger campus. It is not sufficient to merely check the box of attending a safe zone ally training. Institutional change requires collaboration, coalition-building, education/training, and continual efforts. In the next section, I highlight a model for creating tangible, institutional change at colleges and universities.

Institutional Change Efforts

Squire and Beck's (2016) *Developmental Pathways to Trans Inclusion on College Campuses,* focuses on creating success and improving the campus environment for trans collegians. While this model focuses on students who hold minoritized gender identities, it holds utility and transferability for other minoritized identities, including minoritized sexual identities. They charged scholar–practitioners to think across three forms of development: individual, organizational, and systemic. Further, they called for examining this development across three levels: getting started (education), going deeper (personal action), and inclusive excellence (advocacy). Their monograph provides tangible suggestions for practitioners to use at their own institutions. Table 6.1 highlights the various forms of development across the three levels in matrix form, as well as examples from each of the levels and forms.

Campus Pride Index

Despite the critiques provided throughout this book, I encourage all institutions to complete the CPI. Some of these critiques, including those focused on the types of institution opting to participate, could be alleviated with greater institutional representation. Further, the questions on the Campus Pride Index, the largest national, institutional-level reporting tool to benchmark LGBTQ resources, can be a helpful starting place for college administrators, faculty, and staff to consider LGBTQ+ inclusive practices. If, for example, an institution does not already provide training on LGBTQ+ issues for admissions staff, seeing that item within the CPI could spark conversation about why it is missing on their campus and what it might look like. Garvey, Rankin et al. (2017) described several institutional benefits available to participants, including a specialized institutional report. While these advantages do not erase the CPI's flaws, increased institutional participation and awareness of inclusive practices could allow for a better understanding of the collegiate landscape as well as an increase in inclusive practice on individual campuses.

Pathways to Creating Inclusive Campus Environments

Institutions should seek to increase the visibility of trans and LGBQ students on campus while seeking to normalize their identities and experiences. Specific strategies for accomplishing this broad goal include:

- allowing students to self-identify on inclusive student records;

- collecting inclusive demographic data for students, including gender and sexuality;

- creating and supporting LGBTQ+ student organizations;

Table 6.1

Matrix Summarizing Squire and Beck's (2016) Model for Trans Inclusion

	Individual	**Organizational**	**Systemic**
Getting started	Self-awareness; use pronouns in introductions; remove gendered language from course materials	Add gender identity, specifically TGNC identities, to protected groups at the institution; update data systems and records to include inclusive options beyond the binary; train campus safety officers on concerns of the trans community	Work to ensure health coverage includes trans health care; use connections to advocate for inclusive records within educational systems
Going deeper	Facilitate and provide space for trans programming; create and support trans organizations	Train others to use inclusive practice; continually assess climate for trans students	Form coalitions and connections with local K-12 schools to garner widespread support; identify organizations in area that serve trans students and create a coalition
Inclusive excellence	Encourage colleagues across campus to review websites and promotional material for problematic language; help identify gender-inclusive restrooms on campus; make information available campuswide	Provide strategies for campus constituents to make resources easily accessible	Advocate for inclusive policies; extend your work beyond campus to include local, state, and federal governments and neighborhoods

Note. Adapted from Squire and Beck's (2016) *Developmental Pathways to Trans Inclusion on College Campuses.*

- creating educational opportunities for faculty, staff, and administrators to learn about LGBTQ+ identities and issues;
- creating positive institutional change on campus for LGBTQ+ students;
- deconstructing genderism on campus;
- focusing efforts on LGBTQ+ alumni giving;
- having a LGBQ+ resource center that is trans inclusive;

- implementing inclusive language on campus;
- providing digital resources for prospective and current LGBTQ+ students;
- providing inclusive LGBTQ+ health care; and
- recruiting LGBTQ+ students.

Even though research suggests LGBTQ+ students are resilient, an unwelcoming or hostile campus creates an added burden to overcome in navigating academic and social spaces in college. Strategies for improving campus climate include the following:

- acknowledging the intersection of sexual and gender identities with other social identities in supporting students;
- creating gender-inclusive housing options;
- creating an inclusive classroom climate;
- including LGBTQ+ related topics within courses and allowing students to write on issues specific to LGBTQ+ populations;
- including readings by LGBTQ+ authors on class syllabi;
- making sense of the ways campus climate affects LGBTQ+ students;
- considering the role of multiple social identities when planning and facilitating campus events;
- considering the ways microaggressions, homophobia, and transphobia exist within campus online settings;
- reducing microaggressions within classrooms and on campus, and;
- understanding that LGBTQ+ students do not necessarily consider campus climate as exclusively negative.

Integrating gender and sexuality into understandings of themselves as students, future employees, romantic partners, and spiritual beings, among other identities, are important tasks for many college students but may be fraught for those with minoritized identities. Strategies for supporting the identity development of LGBTQ+ students include the following:

- acknowledging the intersectional nature of oppressed identities,
- actively recruiting LGBTQ+ students,
- considering the role of identity development within all contexts of campus,
- creating affirming spaces for LGBTQ+ students,

- developing pathways for LGBTQ+ students to create kinship networks on campus,

- discussing microaggressions and non-inclusive language when they occur within classroom settings,

- training all campus employees (i.e., faculty, staff, administrators) to be sources of support for LGBTQ+ students,

- understanding that identity is fluid,

- understanding the role of institution type in LGBTQ+ students' experiences on campus, and

- working with K-12 school counselors to support prospective LGBTQ+ students.

Final Call to Action

I end this book with a question: Now what? If as educators, we are committed to the success of all students, how will we use the tools highlighted within this text to create tangible, long-lasting, and inclusive change for queer and trans college students? LGBTQ+ students are relying on us to be the change they need. Will we be there them? How will we respond?

References

Abes, E. S., & Kasch, D. (2007). Using queer theory to explore lesbian college students' multiple dimensions of identity. *Journal of College Student Development, 48*(6), 619-636.

ACPA-College Student Educators International/NASPA-National Association of Student Personnel Administrators. (2015). *Professional competency areas for student affairs educators.*

Alessi, E. J., Sapiro, B., Kahn, S., & Craig, S. L. (2017). The first-year university experience for sexual minority students: A grounded theory exploration. *Journal of LGBT Youth, 14*(1), 71-92.

Astin, A .W. (1977). *Four critical years.* Jossey-Bass.

Baum, B. S. (2012, Fall). LGBT applicants and challenges for admission: Five cases. *Journal of College Admission,* 24-29.

Bazarky, D., Morrow, L. K., & Javier, G. C. (2015). Cocurricular and campus contexts. *New Directions for Student Services, 152,* 55-71.

Beemyn, G. (2012). The experiences and needs of transgender community college students. *Community College Journal of Research and Practice, 36*(7), 504-510.

Beemyn, G. (2015). Raising and empowering LGBTQ and gender-nonconforming youth. *Transgender Studies Quarterly, 2*(4), 720-724.

Beemyn, G., & Brauer, D. (2015). Trans-inclusive college records: Meeting the needs of an increasingly diverse U.S. student population. *Transgender Studies Quarterly, 2*(3), 478-487.

Beemyn, G., & Rankin, S. (2011). Introduction to the special issue on "LGBTQ campus experiences." *Journal of Homosexuality, 58*(9), 1159-1164.

Beemyn, G., & Rankin, S. (2016). Creating a gender-inclusive campus. In Y. Martinez-San Miguel & S. Tobias (Eds.), *Trans studies: The challenge to hetero/homo normativities* (pp. 21-32). Rutgers University Press.

Benitez, M., Jr. (2010). Resituating culture centers within a social justice framework: Is there room for examining Whiteness? In L. D. Patton (Ed.), *Culture centers in higher education: Perspectives on identity, theory, and practice* (pp. 119-134). Stylus.

Bilodeau, B. L., & Renn, K. A. (2005). Analysis of LGBT identity development models and implications for practice. *New Directions for Student Services, 111,* 25-39.

Bennett, L. A. (2019). *"Counted and seen": Complicating the governance of (A) gender (s) by university registrar practices* [Doctoral dissertation, The University of Alabama].

Bowden, R., & McCauley, K. (2016). Leadership styles of college and university athletic directors and the presence of NCAA transgender policy. *Journal of Educational Issues, 2*(2), 267-289.

Bowerman, M. (2016, October 12). What does it mean to be pansexual? *USA Today.* https://www.usatoday.com/story/life/nation-now/2016/10/12/miley-cyrus-what-does-mean-pansexual-glaad-questions/91944906/

Braquet, D. (2019). LGBTQ+ terminology, scenarios and strategies, and relevant web-based resources in the 21st century: A glimpse. In B. Mehra (Ed.), *LGBTQ+ librarianship in the 21st century: Emerging directions of advocacy and community engagement in diverse information environments* (pp. 49-61). Emerald Publishing Limited.

Brauer, D. (2017). Complexities of supporting transgender students' use of self-identified first names and pronouns. *College & University, 92*(3), 2-13.

Bronfenbrenner, U. (1993). The ecology of cognitive development: Research models and fugitive findings. In R. H. Wozniak & K. W. Fischer (Eds.), *Development in context: Acting and thinking in specific environments.* Erlbaum.

Buchmann, C., & DiPrete, T. A. (2006). The growing female advantage in college completion: The role of parental resources and academic achievement. *American Sociological Review, 71*(4), 515-541.

Burns, T. (2016, December 9). What you need to know the difference between bisexual and pansexual. *Your Tango.* https://www.yourtango.com/2016298173/the-big-difference-between-pansexual-and-bisexual

Butler, J. (1990). *Gender trouble: Feminism and the subversion of identity.* Routledge.

Butler, J. (2014). *Bodies that matter: On the discursive limits of "sex."* Routledge.

Calvacante, A. (2019). Tumbling into queer utopias and vortexes: Experiences of LGBTQ social media users on Tumblr. *Journal of Homosexuality, 66*(12), 1715-1735.

Campus Pride. (2018). *National Listing of LGBTQ-Friendly Colleges & Universities* [Data file]. Retrieved February 2018 from https://www.campusprideindex.org/searchresults/display/0

Campus Pride. (n.d.-a). *About us.* https://www.campusprideindex.org/menu/aboutus

Campus Pride. (n.d.-b). *Frequently asked questions.* https://www.campusprideindex.org/faqs/index

Campus Pride. (n.d.-c). *Trans Policy Clearinghouse.* https://www.campuspride.org/tpc/

Carter, B. A. (2013). "Nothing better or worse than being Black, gay, and in the band": A qualitative examination of gay undergraduates participating in historically Black college or university marching bands. *Journal of Research in Music Education, 61*(1), 26-43.

Case, K. A., Kanenberg, H., Erich, S. A., & Tittsworth, J. (2012). Transgender inclusion in university nondiscrimination statements: Challenging gender-conforming privilege through student activism. *Journal of Social Issues, 68*(1), 145-161.

Cegler, T. D. (2012, Spring). Targeted recruitment of GLBT students by colleges and universities. *Journal of College Admission, 215,* 18-23.

Consortium of Higher Education LGBT Resource Professionals. (2016). *2016 Annual Report.* https://issuu.com/lgbtcampus/docs/board_report_2016_ver4_final

Cramer, E. P., & Ford, C. H. (2011). Gay rights on campus, circa 2011. *Academe, 97*(5).

Crowhurst, M., & Emslie, M. (2014). Counting queers on campus: Collecting data on queerly identifying students. *Journal of LGBT Youth, 11*(3), 276-288.

Davy, Z., Amsler, S., & Duncombe, K. (2015). Facilitating LGBT medical, health and social care content in higher education teaching. *Qualitative Research in Education, 4*(2), 134-163.

Deniz, C. (2017). Reconceptualization sexuality and rethinking homophobia in metropolitan campus spaces. *Journal for Critical Education Policy Studies, 15*(1), 228-251.

Denton, J. M. (2016). Critical and poststructural perspectives on sexual identity formation. *New Directions for Student Services, 154,* 57-69.

Dessel, A. B., Goodman, K. D., & Woodford, M. R. (2017). LGBT discrimination on campus and heterosexual bystanders: Understanding intentions to intervene. *Journal of Diversity in Higher Education, 10*(2), 101-116.

Dilley, P. (2010). New century, new identities: Building on a typology of nonheterosexual college men. *Journal of LGBT Youth, 7,* 186-199.

Dillon, F. R., Worthington, R. L., & Moradi, B. (2011). Sexual identity as a universal process. In S. J. Schwartz, K. Luyckx, & V. L. Vignoles (Eds.), *Handbook of identity theory and research* (pp. 649-670). Springer.

Dirks, D. A. (2016). Transgender people at four Big Ten campuses: A policy discourse analysis. *The Review of Higher Education, 39*(3), 371-393.

Dugan, J. P., Kusel, M. L., & Simounet, D. M. (2012). Transgender college students: An exploratory study of perceptions, engagement, and educational outcomes. *Journal of College Student Development, 53*(5), 719-736.

Dugan, J. P., & Yurman, L. (2011). Commonalities and differences among lesbian, gay, and bisexual college students: Considerations for research and practice. *Journal of College Student Development, 52*(2), 201-216.

Duran, A. (2018). Queer and of color: A systemic literature review of queer students of color in higher education scholarship. *Journal of Diversity in Higher Education.* Advance online publication. http://dx.doi.org/10.1037/dhe0000084

Duran, A., & Nicolazzo, Z. (2017). Exploring the ways trans* collegians navigate academic, romantic, and social relationships. *Journal of College Student Development, 58*(4), 526-544.

Feldman, D. C. (1976). A contingency theory of socialization. *Administrative Science Quarterly, 21,* 433-452.

Fine, L. E. (2012). The context of creating space: Assessing the likelihood of college LGBT center presence. *Journal of College Student Development, 53*(2), 285-299.

Fine, L. E. (2015). Penalized or privileged? Sexual identity, gender, and postsecondary educational attainment. *American Journal of Education, 121,* 271-297.

Friedman, C., & Leaper, C. (2010). Sexual-minority college women's experiences with discrimination: Relations with identity and collective action. *Psychology of Women Quarterly, 34,* 152-164.

Furrow, H. (2012). LGBT students in the college composition classroom. *Journal of Ethnographic and Qualitative Research, 6,* 145-159.

Garvey, J. C. (2016). Conceptualization and validation of factors for LGBTQ alumni philanthropy. *Journal of College Student Development, 57*(6), 748-754.

Garvey, J. C. (2017). Considerations for queer as a sexual identity classification in education survey research. *Journal of College Student Development, 58*(7), 1113-1118.

Garvey, J. C., & Drezner, N. D. (2013). Advancement staff and alumni advocates: Cultivating LGBTQ alumni by promoting individual and community uplift. *Journal of Diversity in Higher Education, 6*(3), 199-218.

Garvey, J. C., & Drezner, N. D. (2019). Towards a culturally inclusive understanding of alumnx philanthropy: The influence of student involvements and experiences on LGBTQ alumnx giving [Supplement]. *Review of Higher Education, 42,* 363-392.

Garvey, J. C., Hart, J., Metcalfe, A. S., Fellabaum-Toston, J. (2019). Methodological troubles with gender and sex in higher education survey research. *The Review of Higher Education, 43*(1), 1-24.

Garvey, J. C., & Inkelas, K. K. (2012). Exploring relationships between sexual orientation and satisfaction with faculty and staff interactions. *Journal of Homosexuality, 59,* 1167-1190.

Garvey, J. C., Matsumura, J. L., Silvis, A., Kiemele, R., Eagan, H., & Chowdury, P. (2018). Sexual borderlands: Exploring outness among bisexual, pansexual, and sexually fluid undergraduate students. *Journal of College Student Development, 59*(6), 666-680.

Garvey, J. C., Mobley, Jr., S. D., Summerville, K. S., & Moore, G. T. (2019). Queer and trans* students of color: Navigating identity disclosure and college contexts. *The Journal of Higher Education, 90*(1), 150-178.

Garvey, J. C., & Rankin, S. R. (2015). Making the grade? Classroom climate for LGBTQ students across gender conformity. *Journal of Student Affairs Research and Practice, 52*(2), 190-203.

Garvey, J. C., Rankin, S., Beemyn, G., & Windmeyer, S. (2017). Improving the campus climate for LGBTQ students using the Campus Pride Index. In K. M. Goodman & D. Cole (Eds.), *Using data-informed decision making to improve student affairs practice* (pp. 61-70). Jossey-Bass.

Garvey, J. C., Sanders, L. A., & Flint, M. A. (2017). Generational perceptions of campus climate among LGBTQ undergraduates. *Journal of College Student Development, 58*(6), 795-817.

Garvey, J. C., Taylor, J. L., & Rankin, S. (2015). An examination of campus climate for LGBTQ community college students. *Community College Journal of Research and Practice, 39*(6), 527-541.

Githens, R. P. (2012). Approaches to diversity in educating for LGBTQ-friendly changes in a university. *Journal of Diversity in Higher Education, 5*(4), 207-221.

GLAAD. (n.d.). *GLAAD media reference guide.* https://www.glaad.org/reference/lgbtq

Grant, J. E., Odlaug, B. L., Derbyshire, K., Schreiber, L. R. N., Lust, K., & Christenson, G. (2014). Mental health and clinical correlates in lesbian, gay, bisexual, and queer young adults. *Journal of American College Health, 62*(1), 75-78.

Hardiman, R., Jackson, B., & Griffin, P. (2007). Conceptual foundations for social justice courses. In M. Adams, L. A. Bell, & P. Griffin (Eds.), *Teaching for diversity and social justice* (2nd ed., pp. 35-66). Routledge.

Hart, J., & Lester, J. (2011). Starring students: Gender performance at a women's college. *NASPA Journal About Women in Higher Education, 4*(2), 193-217.

Hughes, B. E. (2017). "Managing by not managing": How gay engineering students manage sexual orientation identity. *Journal of College Student Development, 58*(3), 385-401.

Hughes, B. E. (2018a). Resilience of grassroots leaders involved in the LGBT issues at a Catholic university. *Journal of Student Affairs Research and Practice, 55*(2), 123-136.

Hughes, B. E. (2018b). Coming out in STEM: Factors affecting retention of sexual minority STEM students. *Science Advances, 4*(3), 1-5.

Hughes, B. E., & Hurtado, S. (2018). Thinking about sexual orientation: College experiences that predict identity salience. *Journal of College Student Development, 59*(3), 309-326.

Human Rights Campaign. (n.d.). *Lavender graduation.* https://www.hrc.org/resources/lavender-graduation

Hurtado, S., & Carter, D. F. (1997). Effects of college transition and perceptions of the campus racial climate on Latino college students' sense of belonging. *Sociology of Education, 70*(4), 324-345.

Ivory, B. T. (2012). Little known, much needed: Addressing the cocurricular needs of LGBTQ students. *Community College Journal of Research and Practice, 36,* 482-493.

Jackson, K. (2016). Supporting LGBTQ students in high school for the college transition: The role of school counselors. *Professional School Counseling, 20*(1a), 21-28.

Jaekel, K. S. (2015). Recommendations from the field: Creating an LGBTQ learning community. *Learning Communities Research and Practice, 3*(2), 1-7.

Jaekel, K. S. (2016). Innovations in teaching: How novice teaching assistants include LGBTQ topics in the writing classroom. *The Journal of Effective Teaching, 16*(1), 89-101.

James, S. E., Herman, J. L., Rankin, S., Keisling, M., Mottet, L., & Anafi, M. (2016). *The Report of the 2015 U.S. Transgender Survey.* National Center for Transgender Equality.

Johnson, R. B., Oxendine, S., Taub, D. J., & Robertson, J. (2013) Suicide prevention for LGBT students. In D. J. Taub & J. Robertson (Eds.), *Preventing college student suicide* (pp. 55-69). Jossey-Bass.

Jones, S. R., & Stewart, D.-L. (2016). Evolution of student development theory. In E. S. Abes (Eds.), *Critical perspectives on student development theory* (New Directions for Student Services, No. 154, pp. 17-28). Wiley.

Kennesaw State. (n.d.). *Stonewall housing.* https://lgbtq.kennesaw.edu/initiatives-services/housing.php

Kilgo, C. A., Linley, J. L., Renn, K. A., & Woodford, M. R. (2019). High-impact for whom? The influence of identity and environment on lesbian, gay, bisexual, and queer college students' participation in high-impact practices. *Journal of College Student Development, 60*(4), 421-436.

Kirsch, A. C., Conley, C. S., & Riley, T. J. (2015). Comparing psychosocial adjustment across the college transition in a matched heterosexual and lesbian, gay, and bisexual sample. *Journal of College Student Development, 56*(2), 155-169.

Knutson, D., Koch, J. M., & Goldbach, C. (2019). Recommended terminology, pronouns, and documentation for work with transgender and non-binary people. *Practice Innovations.* Advanced online publication. http://dx.doi.org/10.1037/pri0000098

Kosciw, J. G., Greytak, E. A., Giga, N. M., Villenas, C., & Danischewski, D. J. (2016). *The 2015 National School Climate Survey: The experiences of lesbian, gay, bisexual, transgender, and queer youth in our nation's schools.* GLSEN.

Krum, T. E., Davis, K. S., & Galupo, M. P. (2013). Gender-inclusive housing preferences: A survey of college-aged transgender students. *Journal of LGBT Youth, 10,* 64-82.

Kuh, G. D. (1990). Assessing student culture. *New Directions for Institutional Research, 68,* 47-60.

Kuh, G. D., Kinzie, J., Schuh, J. H., & Whitt, E. J. (2005). *Student success in college: Creating conditions that matter.* Jossey-Bass.

Legg, K., Cofino, A., & Sanlo, R. (2020). Lesbian, gay, bisexual, and transgender college students: Revisiting retention. *Journal of College Student Retention: Research, Theory, and Practice, 21*(4), 417-430.

Lennon, E., & Mistler, B. J. (2014). Cisgenderism. *Transgender Studies Quarterly, 1*(1-2), 63-64.

Lewis & Clark College. (n.d.). *LGBTQ career resource guide.* https://college.lclark.edu/student_life/career_development/for_students/job_search_planning/lgbtq_career_resources.php

Linley, J. L. (2017). We are (not) all bulldogs: Minoritized peer socialization agents' meaning-making about collegiate contexts. *Journal of College Student Development, 58*(5), 643-656.

Linley, J. L., & Kilgo, C. A. (2018). Expanding agency: Centering gender identity in college and university student record systems. *Journal of College Student Development, 59*(3), 359-365.

Linley, J. L., & Nguyen, D. J. (2015). LGBT experiences in curricular contexts. In D.-L. Stewart, K. A. Renn, & G. B. Brazelton (Eds.), *Gender and sexual diversity in U.S. higher education: Contexts and opportunities for LGBTQ college students* (pp. 41-53). Jossey-Bass.

Linley, J. L., Nguyen, D., Brazelton, G. B., Becker, B., Renn, K., & Woodford, M. (2016). Faculty as sources of support for LGBTQ college students. *College Teaching, 64*(2), 55-63.

Manning, P., Pring, L., & Glider, P. (2012). Relevance of campus climate for alcohol and other drug use among LGBTQ community college students: A statewide qualitative assessment. *Community College Journal of Research and Practice, 36*(7), 494-503.

Marine, S. B., & Nicolazzo, Z. (2014). Names that matter: Exploring the tensions of campus LGBTQ centers and trans* inclusion. *Journal of Diversity in Higher Education, 7*(4), 265-281.

Martin, G., Broadhurst, C., Hoffshire, M., & Takewell, W. (2018). "Students at the margins": Student affairs administrators creating inclusive campuses for LGBTQ students in the South. *Journal of Student Affairs Research and Practice, 55*(1), 1-13.

Mathis, D., & Tremblay, C. (2010). Pride on the other side: The emergence of LGBT web sites for prospective students. *College and University, 86*(1), 45-50.

Mayhew, M. J., Rockenbach, A. N., Bowman, N. A., Seifert, T. A., & Wolniak, G. C. (2016). *How college affects students: 21st century evidence that higher education works* (Vol. 3). Jossey-Bass.

McEntarfer, H. K. (2011). "Not going away": Approaches used by students, faculty, and staff members to create gay–straight alliances at three religiously affiliated universities. *Journal of LGBT Youth, 8,* 309-331.

Means, D. R. (2017). "Quaring" spirituality: The spiritual counterstories and spaces of Black gay and bisexual male college students. *Journal of College Student Development, 58*(2), 229-246.

Milem, J. F., Chang, M. J., & Antonio, A. L. (2005). *Making diversity work on campus: A research-based perspective.* American Association of Colleges and Universities.

Miller, R. A. (2015). "Sometimes you feel invisible": Performing queer/disabled in the university classroom. *The Educational Forum, 79*(4), 377-393.

Miller, R. A. (2017). "My voice is definitely strongest in online communities": Students using social media for queer and disability identity-making. *Journal of College Student Development, 58*(4), 509-525.

Mobley, Jr., S. D., & Hall, L. (2020). (Re)defining queer and trans* student retention and "success" at historically Black colleges and universities. *Journal of College Student Retention: Research, Theory, & Practice, 21*(4), 497-519.

Mobley, Jr., S. D., & Johnson, J. M. (2015). The role of HBCUs in addressing the unique needs of LGBT students. In R. T. Palmer, C. R. Shorette II, & M. Gasman (Eds.), *Exploring diversity at historically Black colleges and universities: Implications for policy and practice* (pp. 79-89). Jossey-Bass.

Mollet, A. L. (2020). "I have a lot of feelings, just none of them in the genitalia region": A grounded theory of asexual college students' identity journeys. *Journal of College Student Development, 61*(2), 189-206.

Mollet, A. L., & Lackman, B. R. (2018). Asexual borderlands: Asexual collegians' reflections on inclusion under the LGBTQ umbrella. *Journal of College Student Development, 59*(5), 623-628.

Museus, S. D. (2014). The Culturally Engaging Campus Environments (CECE) Model: A new theory of college success among racially diverse student populations. In M. B. Paulsen (Ed.), *Higher education: Handbook of theory and research* (Vol. 29, pp. 189-227). Springer. http://doi.org/dwdv

Nagoshi, C. T., Cloud, J. R., Lindley, L. M., Nagoshi, J., & Lothamer, L. J. (2019). A test of the three-component model of gender-based prejudices: Homophobia and Transphobia are affected by raters' and targets' assigned at birth. *Sex Roles, 80*, 137-146.

National Center for Educational Statistics. (n.d.). *IPEDS 2018-19 data collection system.* Retrieved from https://surveys.nces.ed.gov/ipeds/

Newhouse, M. R. (2013, Summer). Remembering the "T" in LGBT: Recruiting and supporting transgender students. *Journal of College Admission*, 22-27.

Nguyen, D. J., Brazelton, G. B., Renn, K. A., & Woodford, M. R. (2018). Exploring the availability and influence of LGBTQ+ student services resources on student success at community colleges: A mixed methods analysis. *Community College Journal of Research and Practice, 42*(11), 783-796.

Nicolazzo, Z. (2016a). "Just go in looking good": The resilience, resistance, and kinship-building of trans* college students. *Journal of College Student Development, 57*(5), 538-556.

Nicolazzo, Z. (2016b). *Trans* in college: Transgender students' strategies for navigating campus life and the institutional politics of inclusion.* Stylus.

Nicolazzo, Z. (2016c). "It's a hard line to walk": Black non-binary trans* collegians' perspectives on passing, realness, and trans*-normativity. *International Journal of Qualitative Studies in Education, 29*(9), 1173-1188.

Nicolazzo, Z., Pitcher, E. N., Renn, K. A., & Woodford, M. (2017). An exploration of trans* kinship as a strategy for student success. *International Journal of Qualitative Studies in Education, 30*(3), 305-319.

North Carolina Central University (NCCU). (n.d.). *LGBTA Resource Center.* https://www.nccu.edu/life-nc-central/health-and-well-being/lgbta-center

Office of the University Registrar. (n.d.). *Graduation requirements and diplomas.* Retrieved from https://www.umass.edu/registrar/students/diploma-and-graduation/graduation-requirements-diplomas

Okanlawon, K. (2017). Homophobic bullying in Nigerian schools: The experiences of LGBT university students. *Journal of LGBT Youth, 14*(1), 51-70.

Olive, J. L. (2015). The impact of friendship on the leadership identity development of lesbian, gay, bisexual, and queer students. *Journal of Leadership Education, 14*(1) 142-159.

Osei-Kofi, N., Shahjahan, R. A., & Patton, L. D. (2010). Centering social justice in the study of higher education: The challenges and possibilities for institutional change. *Equity & Excellence in Education, 43*(3), 326-340.

Ottenritter, N. (2012). Crafting a caring and inclusive environment for LGBTQ community college students, faculty, and staff. *Community College Journal of Research and Practice, 36*(7), 531-538.

Pascarella, E. T., & Terenzini, P. T. (2005). *How college affects students: A third decade of research.* Jossey-Bass.

Patton, L. D., Renn, K. A., Guido, F. M, & Quaye, S. J. (2016). *Student development in college: Theory, research, and practice.* Jossey-Bass.

Pharr, S. (1997). *Homophobia: A weapon of sexism.* Chardon Press.

Pitcher, E. N., Camacho, T. P., Renn, K. A., & Woodford, M. R. (2018). Affirming policies, programs, and supportive services: Using an organizational perspective to understand LGBTQ+ college student success. *Journal of Diversity in Higher Education, 11*(2), 117-132.

Preston, M. J., & Hoffman, G. D. (2015). Traditionally heterogendered institutions: Discourses surrounding LGBTQ college students. *Journal of LGBT Youth, 12*(1), 64-86.

Pryor, J. T. (2015). Out in the classroom: Transgender student experiences at a large public university. *Journal of College Student Development, 56*(5), 440-455.

Pryor, J. T., Garvey, J. C., & Johnson, S. (2017). Pride and progress? 30 years of ACPA and NASPA LGBTQ presentations. *Journal of Student Affairs Research and Practice, 54*(2), 123-136.

Pryor, J. T., Ta, D., & Hart, J. (2016). Searching for home: Transgender students and experiences with residential housing. *College Student Affairs Journal, 34*(2), 43-59.

Rankin, S., & Garvey, J. C. (2015). Identifying, quantifying, and operationalizing queer-spectrum students: Assessment and research in student affairs. *New Directions for Student Services, 152,* 73-84.

Rankin, S., & Reason, R. (2008). Transformational tapestry model: A comprehensive approach to transforming campus climate. *Journal of Diversity in Higher Education, 1*(4), 262-274.

Rankin, S., Weber, G., Blumenfeld, W., & Frazer, S. (2010). *2010 state of higher education for lesbian, gay, bisexual, and transgender people.* Campus Pride.

Renn, K. A. (2007). LGBT student leaders and queer activists: Identities of lesbian, gay, bisexual, transgender, and queer identified college student leaders and activists. *Journal of College Student Development, 48*(3), 311-330.

Renn, K. A. (2010). LGBT and queer research in higher education: The state and status of the field. *Educational Researcher, 39*(2), 132-141.

Renn, K. A., & Arnold, K. D. (2003). Reconceptualizing research on college student peer culture. *The Journal of Higher Education, 74*(3), 261-291.

Renn, K. A., & Reason, R. D. (2013). *College students in the United States: Characteristics, experiences, and outcomes.* Jossey-Bass.

Rich, A. (1980). Compulsory heterosexuality and lesbian existence. *Women: Sex and Sexuality, 5*(4), 631-660.

Rivera-Ramos, Z. A., Oswald, R. F., & Buki, L. P. (2015). A Latina/o campus community's readiness to address lesbian, gay, and bisexual concerns. *Journal of Diversity in Higher Education, 8*(2), 88-103.

Rockenbach, A. N., & Crandall, R. E. (2016). Faith and LGBTQ inclusion: Navigating the complexities of the campus spiritual climate in Christian higher education. *Christian Higher Education, 15*(1-2), 62-71.

Rockenbach, A. N., Lo, M. A., & Mayhew, M. J. (2017). How LGBT college students perceive and engage the campus religious and spiritual climate. *Journal of Homosexuality, 64*(4), 488-508.

Rockenbach, A. N., Riggers-Piehl, T. A., Garvey, J. C., Lo, M. A., & Mayhew, M. J. (2016). The influence of campus climate and interfaith engagement on self-authored worldview commitment and pluralism orientation across sexual and gender identities. *Research in Higher Education, 57*, 497-517.

Rubin, H., Erlick, E., Pan, L., Charlie, K, & Worrell, M. (2016). *Comprehensive model policy on transgender students for four-year colleges and universities.* Retrieved from: http://trans-student.org/what-we-do/policy/comprehensive-model-policy-on-transgender-students-for-four-year-colleges-and-universities/

Sanlo, R., & Espinoza, L. (2012). Risk and retention: Are LGBTQ students staying in your community college? *Community College Journal of Research and Practice, 36*(7), 475-481.

Schmidt, C. K., Miles, J. R., & Welsh, A. C. (2011). Perceived discrimination and social support: The influences on career development and college adjustment of LGBT college students. *Journal of Career Development, 38*(4), 293-309.

Schulze, C., & Perkins, W. (2017). Awareness of sexual violence services among LGBQ-identified college students. *Journal of School Violence, 16*(2), 148-159.

Self, J. M., & Hudson, K. D. (2015). Dangerous waters and brave space: A critical feminist inquiry of campus LGBTQ centers. *Journal of Gay & Lesbian Social Services, 27*(2), 216-245.

Smith, K. (2018, February 2). Campus Ministry, Gender Relations to host LGBTQ retreat. *The Observer.* Retrieved from https://ndsmcobserver.com/2018/02/lgbtq-retreat/

Squire, D., & Beck, B. (2016). *Developmental pathways to trans inclusion on college campuses.* ACPA-College Student Educators International.

Squire, D., & Norris, L. (2014). Supporting students in the margins: Establishing a first-year experience for LGBTQA students. *Journal of Student Affairs Research and Practice, 51*(2), 195-206.

Stewart, D.-L.(2013). Racially minoritized students at U.S. four-year institutions. *The Journal of Negro Education, 82*(2), 184-197.

Strayhorn, T. L. (2012). *College students' sense of belonging: A key to educational success for all students.* Routledge.

Strayhorn, T. L., & Mullins, T. G. (2012). Investigating Black gay male undergraduates' experiences in campus residence halls. *Journal of College and University Housing, 38/39*(2/1), 140-161.

Stryker, S. (2008). *Transgender history.* Seal Press.

Taylor, J. L. (2015). Call to action: Embracing an inclusive LGBTQ culture on community college campuses. In E. L. Castro (Ed.), *Understanding equity in community college practice* (pp. 57-66). Jossey-Bass.

Taylor, J. L., Dockendorff, K. J., & Inselman, K. (2018). Decoding the digital campus climate for prospective LGBTQ+ community college students. *Community College Journal of Research and Practice, 42*(3), 155-170.

Tillapaugh, D. (2015). Critical influences on sexual minority college males' meaning-making of their multiple identities. *Journal of Student Affairs Research and Practice, 52*(1), 64-75.

Tompkins, A. (2014). Asterisk. *TSQ: Transgender Studies Quarterly, 1*(1/2), 26-27.

Trans @ Iowa. (n.d.). *Identity terminology.* Retrieved from https://uiowa.edu/ui-trans-resources/identity-terminology

Trans Student Educational Resources (n.d.). *LGBTQ+ definitions.* Retrieved from http://www.transstudent.org/definitions

UMass Trans FAQ. (n.d.). *Resources.* Retrieved from https://www.umass.edu/stonewall/resources/umass-trans-resource-guiden

University of Notre Dame. (n.d.). *LGBTQ retreat.* Retrieved from https://campusministry.nd.edu/get-involved/retreats-pilgrimages/lgbtq-retreat/

Vaccaro, A. (2012). Campus microclimates for LGBT faculty, staff, and students: An exploration of the intersections of social identity and campus roles. *Journal of Student Affairs Research and Practice, 49*(4), 429-446.

Vaccaro, A., & Newman, B. M. (2017). A sense of belonging through the eyes of first-year LGBPQ students. *Journal of Student Affairs Research and Practice, 54*(2), 137-149.

Vaccaro, A., Russell, E. I. A., & Koob, R. M. (2015). Students with minoritized identities of sexuality and gender in campus contexts: An emergent model. In D.-L. Stewart, K. A. Renn, & G. B. Brazelton (Eds.), *Gender and sexual diversity in U.S. higher education: contexts and opportunities for LGBTQ college students* (pp. 25-39). Jossey-Bass.

Vespone, B. M. (2016). Integrating identities: Facilitating a support group for LGBTQ students on a Christian college campus. *Christian Higher Education, 15*(4), 215-229.

Waling, A., & Roffee, J. A. (2017). Knowing, performing and holding queerness: LGBTIQ+ student experiences in Australian tertiary education. *Sex education: Sexuality, society and learning, 17*(3), 302-318.

Walker, J. J., & Longmire-Avital, B. (2013). The impact of religious faith and internalized homonegativity on resiliency for Black lesbian, gay, and bisexual emerging adults. *Developmental Psychology, 49*(9), 1723-1731.

Watt, S. K. (2015). *Designing transformative multicultural initiatives: Theoretical foundations, practical applications, and facilitator considerations.* Stylus.

White, V., Greenhalgh, M., & Oja, M. (2012). GLADE: Supporting LGBT staff and students in a community college district. *Community College Journal of Research and Practice, 36*(7), 526-530.

Wickens, C. M., & Sandlin, J. A. (2010). Homophobia and heterosexism in a college of education: A culture of fear, a culture of silence. *International Journal of Qualitative Studies in Education, 23*(6), 651-670.

Wilson, B. D. M., Jordan, S. P., Meyer, I. H., Flores, A. R., Stemple, L., & Herman, J. L. (2017). Disproportionality and disparities among sexual minority youth in custody. *Journal of Youth and Adolescence, 46*(7), 1547-1561.

Wolff, J. R., Himes, H. L., Kwon, E. M., & Bollinger, R. A. (2012, July). Evangelical Christian college students and attitudes toward gay rights: A California university sample. *Journal of LGBT Youth, 9*(3), 200-224.

Woodford, M. R., Joslin, J. Y., Pitcher, E. N., & Renn, K. A. (2017). A mixed-methods inquiry into trans* environmental microaggressions on college campuses: Experiences and outcomes. *Journal of Ethnic & Cultural Diversity in Social Work, 26*(1-2), 95-111.

Woodford, M. R., Joslin, J., & Renn, K. A. (2016). Lesbian, gay, bisexual, transgender, and queer students on campus: Fostering inclusion through research, policy, and practice. In P. A. Pasque, N. Ortega, J. C. Burkhardt, & M. P. Ting (Eds.), *Transforming understandings of diversity in higher education* (pp. 57-80). Stylus.

Woodford, M. R., Kolb, C. L., Durocher-Radeka, G., & Javier, G. (2014). Lesbian, gay, bisexual, and transgender ally training programs on campus: Current variations and future directions. *Journal of College Student Development, 55*(3), 317-322.

Woodford, M. R., Kulick, A., & Atteberry, B. (2015). Protective factors, campus climate, and health outcomes among sexual minority college students. *Journal of Diversity in Higher Education, 8*(2), 73-87.

Woodford, M. R., Kulick, A., Sinco, B. R., & Hong, J. S. (2014). Contemporary heterosexism on campus and psychological distress among LGBQ students: The mediating role of self-acceptance. *American Journal of Orthopsychiatry, 84*(5), 519-529.

Woodford, M. R., & Kulick, A. (2015). Academic and social integration on campus among sexual minority students: The impacts of psychological and experiential campus climate. *American Journal of Community Psychology, 55*(1-2), 13-25.

Woodford, M. R., Silverschanz, P., Swank, E., Scherrer, K. S., & Raiz, L. (2012). Predictors of heterosexual college students' attitudes toward LGBT people. *Journal of LGBT Youth, 9,* 297-320.

Woodford, M. R., Weber, G., Nicolazzo, Z., Hunt, R., Kulick, A., Coleman, T., Coulombe, S., & Renn, K. A. (2018). Depression and attempted suicide among LGBTQ college students: Fostering resilience to the effects of heterosexism and cisgenderism on campus. *Journal of College Student Development, 59*(4), 420-436.

Worthen, M. G. F. (2011). College student experiences with an LGBTQ ally training program: A mixed methods study at a university in the southern United States. *Journal of LGBT Youth, 8,* 332-377.

Worthen, M. G. F. (2014). Blaming the jocks and the Greeks? Exploring collegiate athletes' and fraternity/sorority members' attitudes toward LGBT individuals. *Journal of College Student Development, 55*(2), 168-195.

Wright, W. (2006). *Harvard's secret court.* St. Martin's Press.

Young, A. (2011, Winter). Gay students: The latest outreach target at many colleges. *Journal of College Admission,* 39-40.

Zamani-Gallaher, E. M. (2017). Conflating gender and identity: The need for gender-fluid programming in community colleges. *New Directions for Community Colleges, 179,* 89-99.

Zamani-Gallaher, E. M., & Choudhuri, D. D. (2011). A primer on LGBTQ students at community colleges: Considerations for research and practice. In E. M. Cox & J. S. Watson (Eds.), *Marginalized students* (New Directions for Community Colleges No. 155, pp. 35-49). Wiley.

Zamani-Gallaher, E. M., & Choudhuri, D. D. (2016). Tracing LGBTQ community college students' experiences. In C. C. Ozaki & R. L. Spaid (Eds.), *Applying college change theories to student affairs practice* (pp. 47-63). Jossey-Bass.

Index

D

data. *See* institutional data; records systems, university

deadnaming, use of term, 8*t*

deepening and commitment, sexual identity and, 21

deficit-based language in institutional policies, 14

degree attainment. *See also* graduation women with minoritized sexual identities and, 57

demiboy and demigirl, use of terms, 3*t*

demigender, use of term, 2, 3*t*

Department of Education, Title IX funding reports to, 30

depression, LGBQ students and, 18

derogatory language, orientation staff and, 40

Developmental Pathways to Trans Inclusion on College Campuses (Squire and Beck), ix, 64, 65*t*

diffusion, as sexual identity status, 21

digital resources, xiii, 33, 66

Dillon, F. R., 21

diplomas, updating names on, 61

direct action to creative inclusive environments, 20

Dirks, D. A., 50

disabilities, queer and trans people with, studies on, 17

discrimination, response to religion as justification for, ix, 55

diversity, institutional, orientation discussions on, 40

Drezner, N. D., 59–60

Dugan, J. P., 19, 23

Duvall, Jessica, 38

E

early-alert systems, 41

Ellucian's Banner, 24, 26

enrollment forms, 30, 39

environment. *See also* campus climate inclusive, xiv, 40, 52, 64–7 sense of belonging on campus and, 34–5 students' identity development and, 22–3

Espinoza, L., 57

exclusion. *See also* belonging, sense of response to religion as justification for, 55 use of acronyms and, 5

exit interviews, 62

experience. *See also* identity studies/experiences identity and, 16–17

experiential climate, 16

extracurricular experiences. *See* cocurriculum and cocurricular experiences

F

faculty

affirming students' sexual and gender identities, 23

classroom climate and, 44–6

educational opportunities for, on LGBTQ+ identities and issues, 65

heterosexist norms and, 22

LGBTQ+, institutional commitment to, 46–7, 47*f*

LGBTQ+ students interactions with, 48–9

safe classroom environments and, 15

studies on interactions with, 17

training, to support LGBTQ+ students, 67

K

K-12 schools
    public, conservative and Christian, ix–x
    working with, to support prospective
    LGBTQ+ students, 67
Kasch, D., 7
Kennesaw State University (KSU), gender-inclusive living–learning community for LGBTQ+ students, 38
Kilgo, C. A., 30, 50
kinship networks
    creating, for LGBTQ+ students on
    campus, 67
    for trans students, 16–17
Kirsch, A. C., 19, 33, 34
Krum, T. E., 36
Kulick, A., 49

L

Lackman, B. R., 5
language. *See also* honorifics; names, chosen; pronouns, identity-aligned
    deficit-based, in institutional policies, 14
    gendered, in admissions materials, 32
    hate or derogatory, 40
    inclusive, 66
    non-inclusive, in classrooms, 67
    in university policies, trans students
    and, 50
lavender graduation ceremonies, 59
learning communities, 20, 38. *See also* living–learning communities
Lesbian, Gay, Bisexual, Transgender, and Ally (LGBTA) Resource Center, North Carolina Central University, 53
lesbian, use of term, 5*t*
Lewis & Clark College Career Center, 60
LGB (lesbian, gay, bisexual)
    academic outcomes, 19, 57

adjustment to college, 19, 33
faculty/staff interactions with, 48
mental health outcomes and, 18
as social identifier in higher education scholarship, 23–4
use of term, 6*t*
youth incarceration rates, 7
LGBPQ (lesbian, gay, bisexual, pansexual, and queer) students
    first-year perspectives of, 33–4
LGBQ+, use of term, 4, 6
LGBQA+, use of term, 4
LGBQQ (lesbian, gay, bisexual, queer, and questioning) students
    first-year perspectives of, 34
    transition to college studies and, 19
LGBT (lesbian, gay, bisexual, and transgender)
    resource centers, 14
    use of term, 6*t*
"LGBT and Queer Research in Higher Education: The State and Status of the Field" (Renn), 9, 63
LGBTQ
Campus Pride use of, 9*n*
definition of, 6*t*
LGBTQ+ students. *See also* minoritized gender identities; minoritized identities; minoritized sexual identities; prospective LGBTQ+ students
    acronyms describing, 4–6, 5*t*, 6*t*
    admissions materials depictions of, 32
    alumnx group for, 62
    anticipatory socialization and, 29
    campus education programs, 19–20
    challenges as college applicants, 29–31
    in the classroom, 44–7
    college adjustment and, 33–7
    curricular contexts for, 43

M

N

names, chosen
    accessible by faculty/staff, 31
    alumnx outreach and, 62
    classroom use of, 44, 45
    course rosters and, 54
    deadnaming instead of using, *8t*
    institutions allowing use of, 26
    records systems tracking of, xii–xiii
    at UMass-Amherst, 61
nametags, pronouns on, 40
National College Climate Survey (Campus Pride, 2010), 44
National Collegiate Athletic Association (NCAA), 14
National LGBT Alumni Survey, 59
National Longitudinal Survey of Adolescent Health, 19
National Student Affairs Professionals Association (NASPA), 15
Native Americans, Two Spirit, *3t*
Newhouse, M. R., 14, 29–30, 31
Newman, B. M., 33–4
Nguyen, D. J., 44
Nicolazzo, Z., 16–17, 18, 20, 51–2
non-binary, use of term, *3t*
non-binary trans students, Black, 17
non-classroom-specific campus climate studies, 15–16
Norris, L., 35
North Carolina Central University, LGBTA Resource Center, 53

O

The One Project, University of Maryland, College Park, 35
online communities, 51, 66
oppression
    of LGBTQ+ identities, *8t*

privilege and, 6–8
organizational development, Squire and Beck on institutional change and, 64, *65t*
organizational perspectives of climate, 16
orientation, 35, 39–40. *See also* college adjustment
Out in Science, Technology, Engineering, and Mathematics (oSTEM), 58
outcomes. *See also* academic outcomes
    for queer and trans college students, studies on, 13, *13f*, 17–19, 63
    socialization and, 29
outing
    inclusive admissions applications and risk of, 30
    student affairs professionals and, xi
outness. See also being out; coming out
    classroom climate and, 44
    focus on, as development essential, 21
    level of, factors in, 4
    not public during college, alumnx outreach to, 62
overall environmental factors in campus climate studies, 15, 16

P

pansexual, use of term, *5t*
Patton, L. D., 21
peers, classroom experiences and, 45
PeopleSoft Campus Solutions, 24, 26
Perkins, W., 52
persistence. *See also* graduation; retention
    academic outcomes and, 22
    institutional data tracking, 26
    Iowa's TNGC students and, 38
    LGBTQ+ students, investigating, 30
personal narrative, author's, ix–xiv
philanthropic engagement of LGBTQ+ alumnx, 14, 59–60, 62, 65

About the Author

Cindy Ann Kilgo is assistant professor of Higher Education and Student Affairs in the Department of Educational Leadership and Policy Studies at Indiana University. Prior to this appointment, they were assistant professor of Higher Education Administration in the Department of Educational Leadership, Policy and Technology Studies at The University of Alabama. Kilgo's research focuses on high-impact educational practices for minoritized student populations and the use of critical quantitative methods in examining how college affects students. Their research has been published in the *Journal of College Student Development, Higher Education, Research in Higher Education, The Journal of Higher Education, Journal of Student Affairs Research and Practice, Journal of College Orientation and Transition, New Directions for Student Services, New Directions for Institutional Research, and the International Journal of Research on Service-Learning and Community Engagement,* among other publication outlets. Further, their research has been featured in *The Chronicle of Higher Education, Inside Higher Ed,* and *Money Magazine.* Kilgo has frequently served as a consultant to institutions on creating inclusive environments for queer and trans students on college campuses. They completed their Ph.D. in Educational Policy and Leadership Studies (Higher Education and Student Affairs) from the University of Iowa in 2016. Prior to their Ph.D., they attained an M.Ed. in Higher Education and Student Affairs from the University of South Carolina and a B.S. in Psychology from Georgia Southern University.